The Joyful Christian

THE JOYFUL

127 Readings from

CHRISTIAN

C. S. LEWIS

COLLIER BOOKS

Macmillan Publishing Company

NEW YORK

Macmillan Publishing Company
866 Third Avenue, New York, N.Y. 10022

Extracts from *Mere Christianity, The Screwtape Letters, The Problem of
Pain, Miracles,* and *The Abolition of Man* are reprinted by permission
of William Collins Sons & Company Limited. Copyright © Macmillan
Publishing Co., Inc. 1944, 1947. Copyright renewed 1972, 1975. Copyright
© Macmillan Publishing Co., Inc. 1943, 1944, 1945, 1952. Copyright
renewed 1972, 1973. Copyright © Macmillan Publishing Co., Inc. 1947.
Copyright renewed 1975. Published by Macmillan Publishing Co., Inc.
1940, 1943. Published by Macmillan Publishing Co., Inc. 1942, 1943.

Selections from *Letters to Malcolm: Chiefly on Prayer, The Four Loves,
Letters of C. S. Lewis, Reflections on the Psalms,* and *The World's Last
Night and Other Essays* are reprinted by permission of Harcourt Brace
Jovanovich, Inc.; copyright © 1958 by C. S. Lewis; copyright © 1960 by
Helen Joy Lewis; copyright © 1963, 1964, by the Estate of C. S. Lewis
and/or C. S. Lewis; copyright © 1966 by W. H. Lewis and Executors
of C. S. Lewis.

Selections from *A Grief Observed* are reprinted with permission of
The Seabury Press; © 1961 by N. W. Clerk [C. S. Lewis].

Selections from *Christian Reflections, God in the Dock,* and *Letters to an
American Lady* are reprinted with permission of Wm. B. Eerdmans Co.;
copyright © 1967 by the Executors of the Estate of C. S. Lewis;
copyright © 1970 by The Trustees of the Estate of C. S. Lewis;
copyright © 1967 by Wm. B. Eerdmans Publishing Co.

Library of Congress Cataloging in Publication Data
Lewis, C. S. (Clive Staples), 1898-1963.
    The joyful Christian.
    Reprint. Originally published: New York:
Macmillan, 1984.
    Bibliography: p.
    1. Church of England—Collected works.
2. Theology—Collected works—20th century.
3. Christian life—Anglican authors—Collected
works.   I. Title.
[BX5037.L4   1984b]   230'.3   84-23084
ISBN 0-02-086930-4 (pbk.)

First Paperback Edition 1984

10   9   8   7   6   5

The Joyful Christian is also published in a hardcover edition by
Macmillan Publishing Company.

Printed in the United States of America

Contents

CONTENTS

CONTENTS

Foreword

IF SALES ARE signs, then C. S. Lewis is one of the most popular Christian theologians being published in the United
States today. He is already well known for such works as
The Screwtape Letters (1942), a satiric correspondence in
which a senior devil instructs a junior devil on the most
salubrious ways to subvert a Christian; for *The Space Trilogy*
(1938, 1943, 1945), a three-volume adventure into science
fiction; and for *The Chronicles of Narnia* (1950–1956), a
seven-volume sally into children's fiction. But it is the sales
of his lesser-known theological works—*Miracles, The Problem of Pain, Reflections on the Psalms,* and *Letters to Malcolm,
Chiefly on Prayer*—that have increased dramatically in the
1970s.

If sales are souls, then *Mere Christianity* is Lewis's most
influential theological work. Not only have clerics and stu-

dents been reading it since it was published in 1952—parts of it were published in 1942, 1943, and 1944—businessmen and politicians have also been picking it up and allowing it to influence their lives. Perhaps the most dramatic incident happened in 1973. The president of an American electronics firm handed a copy of the work to a lawyer who was then special counsel to the White House. After reading it, praying over it, discussing it with others, Charles W. Colson underwent a conversion to Christ that he was to describe in his best-selling *Born Again*.

Lewis himself was a convert. It happened on the way to a zoo. His brother was driving a motorcycle; he was riding in the sidecar. At the beginning of the trip he did not believe that Jesus Christ was the Son of God. Somewhere along the way—he was not blinded like St. Paul on the road to Damascus nor was he sprung from the sidecar by a piece of piano wire divinely strung across the roadway—he was, as he recounts in his autobiography, "surprised by joy." At the end of the trip he found himself believing what he thought he never could.

That was in 1931. At the time he was teaching English literature and language at Magdalen College, Oxford. In the mornings he would give lectures and tutorials; in the afternoons he would enjoy brisk walks and large cups of tea; in the evenings he would write and study. Some nights he would invite two or three students to his rooms for port, beer, and stimulating talk. One night a week for years he devoted to a group of friends who talked, read their latest compositions, and exchanged personal as well as literary criticisms. Two of his scholarly works have become classics: *The Allegory of Love* and *English Literature in the Sixteenth Century*—and one of his spiritual works got him on the cover of *Time* magazine: *The Screwtape Letters*. In the early 1940s he delivered twenty-five talks on various Christian topics over British radio; in the late 1950s he recorded ten lectures on love for use on American radio. In 1954 he was appointed Professor of Medieval and Renaissance English Literature at Cambridge University, a post he held until shortly before his death.

If there is one word to describe Lewis's life, it would be *joy*. The harmonizing of himself with the rest of the created world, the process that led him from atheism through theism and pantheism to Christianity, he has described as joy. His lectures and books, the ones dealing with things theological, can also be described as a sort of joy in that they attempt to attune the modern intellect to the facts and truths of Christianity. His marriage in 1957 was an intense, if very brief, joy of a different sort; Joy Davidman was her name; she died of cancer three years later. And since 1963, when he died at the age of sixty-five, he has no doubt been about the serious business of heaven, which he fully expected to be joy.

The sort of Christianity Lewis espoused throughout his life can be compared to his taste in food. As described by his brother, "His requirements were simply but strongly felt. Plain, domestic cookery was what he wanted, with the proviso that if the food was hot the plates should be hot as well. What he really disliked was 'messed up food,' by which he meant any sort of elaborately dressed dishes" (*Letters of C. S. Lewis*, 16).

What Lewis disliked about certain Christian doctrines were the elaborately prepared and elegantly served sauces, like transsubstantiation or consubstantiation for the Eucharist. "The command, after all, was Take, eat: not Take, understand" (*Letters to Malcolm*, 104). To him too much definition could disguise or even destroy the basic content of a doctrine. And he noted with distaste the bloodshed in the kitchen where theologians with contrary recipes have been sundering each other for centuries.

Although he thumped and thwacked every Christian communion for some excess of doctrinal enthusiasm, he also praised each of them for having one or another doctrine in its purest form. Discreetly, charitably, he almost never mentioned a denomination by name. Where historical or doctrinal controversies appeared, he was invariably to be found in the extreme middle. It is neither good actions nor faith in Christ that leads a Christian home—that's "like asking which blade of a scissors is [more] necessary" (*Mere Christianity*, 109)—it is both. This plainness, this mereness, of his theology makes him ecumenical *in excelsis* and helps explain why Christians of all sorts respond so enthusiastically to his work.

What a Christian can joyfully believe, therefore, is the subject of this anthology, and selections have been taken from fifteen of C. S. Lewis's works. The readings are thematically arranged, informally systematized, and devotionally styled. Sources of the readings are given at the back of this book; each source is readily available in a paperback edition; the bibliography tells the precise title and appropriate publisher.

With regard to the texts of the readings, no attempt has been made to produce a critical edition. The punctuation has merely been standardized, the spelling Americanized, the Latin abbreviations Englished, and the hyphens no longer deemed necessary by lexicographers deleted. Capitalizations of the divine pronoun and a variety of abstract nouns remain Lewis's own.

—WILLIAM GRIFFIN
Macmillan Publishing Company
July 15, 1977

The Joyful Christian

Right and Wrong

EVERYONE HAS HEARD people quarreling. Sometimes it sounds funny and sometimes it sounds merely unpleasant; but however it sounds, I believe we can learn something very important from listening to the kinds of things they say. They say things like this: "How'd you like it if anyone did the same to you?"—"That's my seat, I was there first"—"Leave him alone, he isn't doing you any harm"—"Why should you shove in first?"—"Give me a bit of your orange, I gave you a bit of mine"—"Come on, you promised." People say things like this every day, educated as well as uneducated, and children as well as grown-ups.

Now what interests me about all these remarks is that the man who makes them is not merely saying that the other man's behavior does not happen to please him. He is appealing to some kind of standard of behavior which he ex-

1

pects the other man to know about. And the other man very seldom replies: "To hell with your standard." Nearly always he tries to make out that what he has been doing does not really go against the standard, or that if it does there is some special excuse. He pretends there is some special reason in this particular case why the person who took the seat first should not keep it, or that things were quite different when he was given the bit of orange, or that something has turned up which lets him off from keeping his promise. It looks, in fact, very much as if both parties had in mind some kind of Law or Rule of fair play, or decent behavior, or morality, or whatever you like to call it, about which they really agreed. And they have. If they had not, they might, of course, fight like animals, but they could not *quarrel* in the human sense of the word. Quarreling means trying to show that the other man is in the wrong. And there would be no sense in trying to do that unless you and he had some sort of agreement as to what Right and Wrong are; just as there would be no sense in saying that a footballer had committed a foul unless there was some agreement about the rules of football.

Now this Law or Rule about Right and Wrong used to be called the Law of Nature. Nowadays, when we talk of the "laws of nature," we usually mean things like gravitation, or heredity, or the laws of chemistry. But when the older thinkers called the Law of Right and Wrong "the Law of Nature," they really meant the Law of *Human* Nature. The idea was that, just as all bodies are governed by the law of gravitation and organisms by biological laws, so the creature called man also had *his* law—with this great difference, that a body could choose either to obey the Law of Human Nature or to disobey it.

The Universe

WE WANT TO KNOW whether the universe simply happens to be what it is for no reason or whether there is a power behind it that makes it what it is. Since that power, if it exists, would be not one of the observed facts but a reality which makes them, no mere observation of the facts can find it. There is only one case in which we can know whether there is anything more, namely our own case, and in that one case we find there is. Or put it the other way round. If there was a controlling power outside the universe, it could not show itself to us as one of the facts inside the universe—no more than the architect of a house could actually be a wall, or staircase, or fireplace in that house. The only way in which we could expect it to show itself would be inside ourselves as an influence or a command trying to get us to behave in a certain way. And that is just what we do find inside ourselves. Surely this ought to arouse our suspicions? In the only case where you can expect to get an answer, the answer turns out to be Yes; and in the other cases, where you do not get an answer, you see why you do not.

Suppose someone asked me, when I see a man in a blue uniform going down the street leaving little paper packets at each house, why I suppose that they contain letters? I should reply, "Because whenever he leaves a similar little packet for me I find it does contain a letter." And if he then objected, "But you've never seen all these letters which you think the other people are getting," I should say, "Of course not, and I shouldn't expect to, because they're not addressed to me. I'm explaining the packets I'm not allowed to open by the ones I'm allowed to open."

It is the same about this question. The only packet I'm allowed to open is Man. When I do, especially when I open that particular man called myself, I find that I do not exist on my own, that I am under a law; that somebody or something wants me to behave in a certain way. I do not, of course, think that if I could get inside a stone or a tree I should find exactly the same thing, just as I do not think all the other people in the street get the same letters as I do. I should expect, for instance, to find that the stone had to obey the law of gravity—that whereas the sender of the letters merely tells me to obey the laws of my human nature, He compels the stone to obey the laws of its stony nature. But I should expect to find that there was, so to speak, a sender in both cases, a Power behind the facts, a Director, a Guide.

Life on Other Planets

I . . . FEAR THE PRACTICAL, not the theoretical, problems which will arise if ever we meet rational creatures which are not human. Against them we shall, if we can, commit all the crimes we have already committed against creatures certainly human but differing from us in features and pigmentation; and the starry heavens will become an object to which good men can look up only with feelings of intolerable guilt, agonized pity, and burning shame.

Of course, after the first debauch of exploitation we shall make some belated attempt to do better. We shall perhaps send missionaries. But can even missionaries be trusted? "Gun and gospel" have been horribly combined in the past.

The missionary's holy desire to save souls has not always been kept quite distinct from the arrogant desire, the busy-body's itch, to (as he calls it) "civilize" the (as he calls them) "natives." Would all our missionaries recognize a fallen race if they met it? Could they? Would they continue to press upon creatures that did not need to be saved that plan of Salvation which God has appointed for Man? Would they denounce as sins mere differences of behavior which the spiritual and biological history of these strange creatures fully justified and which God Himself had blessed? Would they try to teach those from whom they had better learn? I do not know.

What I do know is that here and now, as our only possible practical preparation for such a meeting, you and I should resolve to stand firm against all exploitation and all theological imperialism. It will not be fun. We shall be called traitors to our own species. We shall be hated of almost all men; even of some religious men. And we must not give back one single inch. We shall probably fail, but let us go down fighting for the right side. Our loyalty is due not to our species but to God. Those who are, or can become, His sons, are our real brothers even if they have shells or tusks. It is spiritual, not biological, kinship that counts.

God in Outer Space

THE RUSSIANS, I am told, report that they have not found God in outer space. On the other hand, a good many people in many different times and countries claim to have found God, or been found by God, here on earth.

The conclusion some want us to draw from these data is that God does not exist. As a corollary, those who think they have met Him on earth were suffering from a delusion.

But other conclusions might be drawn.

(1) We have not yet gone far enough in space. There had been ships on the Atlantic for a good time before America was discovered.

(2) God does exist but is locally confined to this planet.

(3) The Russians did find God in space without knowing it because they lacked the requisite apparatus for detecting Him.

(4) God does exist but is not an object either located in a particular part of space nor diffused, as we once thought "ether" was, throughout space.

The first two conclusions do not interest me. The sort of religion for which they could be a defense would be a religion for savages: the belief in a local deity who can be contained in a particular temple, island, or grove. That, in fact, seems to be the sort of religion about which the Russians—or some Russians, and a good many people in the West—are being irreligious. It is not in the least disquieting that no astronauts have discovered a god of that sort. The really disquieting thing would be if they had.

The third and fourth conclusions are the ones for my money. . . .

Space travel really has nothing to do with the matter. To some, God is discoverable everywhere; to others, nowhere. Those who do not find Him on earth are unlikely to find Him in space. (Hang it all, we're in space already; every year we go a huge circular tour in space.) But send a saint up in a spaceship and he'll find God in space as he found God on earth. Much depends on the seeing eye.

Atheism

MY ARGUMENT AGAINST GOD was that the universe seemed so cruel and unjust. But how had I got this idea of *just* and *unjust?* A man does not call a line crooked unless he has some idea of a straight line. What was I comparing this universe with when I called it unjust? If the whole show was bad and senseless from A to Z, so to speak, why did I, who was supposed to be part of the show, find myself in such violent reaction against it? A man feels wet when he falls into water, because man is not a water animal: a fish would not feel wet. Of course, I could have given up my idea of justice by saying it was nothing but a private idea of my own. But if I did that, then my argument against God collapsed too—for the argument depended on saying that the world was really unjust, not simply that it did not happen to please my private fancies. Thus in the very act of trying to prove that God did not exist—in other words, that the whole of reality was senseless—I found I was forced to assume that one part of reality—namely my idea of justice— was full of sense. Consequently atheism turns out to be too simple. If the whole universe has no meaning, we should never have found out that it has no meaning: just as, if there were no light in the universe and therefore no creatures with eyes, we should never know it was dark. *Dark* would be without meaning.

Seeing and Believing

IN ALL MY LIFE I have met only one person who claims to have seen a ghost. And the interesting thing about the story is that that person disbelieved in the immortal soul before she saw the ghost and still disbelieves after seeing it. She says that what she saw must have been an illusion or a trick of the nerves. And obviously she may be right. Seeing is not believing.

For this reason, the question whether miracles occur can never be answered simply by experience. Every event which might claim to be a miracle is, in the last resort, something presented to our senses, something seen, heard, touched, smelled, or tasted. And our senses are not infallible. If anything extraordinary seems to have happened, we can always say that we have been the victims of an illusion. If we hold a philosophy which excludes the supernatural, this is what we always shall say. What we learn from experience depends on the kind of philosophy we bring to experience. It is therefore useless to appeal to experience before we have settled, as well as we can, the philosophical question. If immediate experience cannot prove or disprove the miraculous, still less can history do so. Many people think one can decide whether a miracle occurred in the past by examining the evidence "according to the ordinary rules of historical inquiry." But the ordinary rules cannot be worked until we have decided whether miracles are possible, and if so, how probable they are. For if they are impossible, then no amount of historical evidence will convince us. If they are possible but immensely improbable, then only mathematically demonstrative evidence will convince us: and since history never provides that degree of evidence for any event, history can never convince us that a miracle occurred. If, on the other hand, miracles are not intrinsically improbable, then the existing evidence will be sufficient to convince us that quite a number of miracles have occurred. The result of our historical inquiries thus depends on the philosophical views which we have been holding before we even began to look at the evidence. The philosophical question must therefore come first.

Miracle and the Laws of Nature

THREE CONCEPTIONS of the "Laws" of Nature have been held. (1) That they are mere brute facts, known only by observation, with no discoverable rhyme or reason about them. We know *that* Nature behaves thus and thus; we do not know *why* she does and can see no reason why she should not do the opposite. (2) That they are applications of the law of averages. The foundations of Nature are in the random and lawless. But the numbers of units we are dealing with are so enormous that the behavior of these crowds (like the behavior of very large masses of men) can be calculated with practical accuracy. What we call "impossible events" are events so overwhelmingly improbable—by actuarial standards—that we do not need to take them into account. (3) That the fundamental laws of Physics are really what we call "necessary truths" like the truths of mathematics—in other words, that if we clearly understand what we are saying, we shall see that the opposite would be meaningless nonsense. Thus it is a "law" that when one billiard ball shoves another, the amount of momentum lost by the first ball must exactly equal the amount gained by the second. People who hold that the laws of Nature are necessary truths would say that all we have done is split up the single event into two halves (adventures of ball A, and adventures of ball B) and then discover that "the two sides of the account balance." When we understand this, we see that, of course, they *must* balance. The fundamental laws are in the long run merely statements that every event is itself and not some different event.

It will at once be clear that the first of these three theories gives no assurance against Miracles—indeed no assurance that, even apart from Miracles, the "laws" which we have hitherto observed will be obeyed tomorrow. If we have no notion why a thing happens, then, of course, we know no reason why it should not be otherwise, and therefore have no certainty that it might not some day be otherwise.

The second theory, which depends on the law of averages, is in the same position. The assurance it gives us is of the same general kind as our assurance that a coin tossed a thousand times will not give the same result, say, nine hundred times: and that the longer you toss it, the more nearly the numbers of Heads and Tails will come to being equal. But this is so only provided the coin is an honest coin. If it is a loaded coin, our expectations may be disappointed. But the people who believe in miracles are maintaining precisely that the coin *is* loaded. The expectation based on the law of averages will work only for *undoctored* Nature. And the question whether miracles occur is just the question whether Nature is ever doctored.

The third view (that Laws of Nature are necessary truths) seems at first sight to present an insurmountable obstacle to miracle. The breaking of them would, in that case, be a self-contradiction and not even Omnipotence can do what is self-contradictory. Therefore the Laws cannot be broken. And therefore, shall we conclude, no miracle can ever occur?

Morality

THERE IS A STORY about a schoolboy who was asked what he thought God was like. He replied that, as far as he could make out, God was "The sort of person who is always snooping round to see if anyone is enjoying himself and then trying to stop it." And I'm afraid that is the sort of idea that the word Morality raises in a good many people's minds: something that interferes, something that stops you having a good time. In reality, moral rules are directions for running the human machine. Every moral rule is there to prevent a breakdown, or a strain, or a friction, in the running of that machine. That is why these rules at first seem to be constantly interfering with our natural inclinations. When you are being taught how to use any machine, the instructor keeps on saying, "No, don't do it like that," because, of course, there are all sorts of things that look all right and seem to you the natural way of treating the machine, but do not really work.

Some people prefer to talk about moral "ideals" rather than moral rules and about moral "idealism" rather than moral obedience. Now it is, of course, quite true that moral perfection is an "ideal" in the sense that we cannot achieve it. In that sense every kind of perfection is, for us humans, an ideal; we cannot succeed in being perfect car drivers or perfect tennis players or in drawing perfectly straight lines. But there is another sense in which it is very misleading to call moral perfection an ideal. When a man says that a certain woman, or house, or ship, or garden is "his ideal," he does not mean (unless he is rather a fool) that everyone else ought to have the same ideal. In such matters we are entitled to have different tastes and, therefore, different ideals. But it is dangerous to describe a man who tries very hard to keep the moral law as a "man of high ideals" because this might lead you to think that moral perfection was a private taste of his own and that the rest of us were not called on to share it. This would be a dangerous mistake.

Perfect behavior may be as unattainable as perfect gear-changing when we drive; but it is a necessary ideal prescribed for all men by the very nature of the human machine just as perfect gear-changing is an ideal prescribed for all drivers by the very nature of cars. And it would be even more dangerous to think of oneself as a person "of high ideals" because one is trying to tell no lies at all (instead of only a few lies), or never to commit adultery (instead of committing it only seldom), or not to be a bully (instead of being only a moderate bully). It might lead you to become a prig and to think you were rather a special person who deserved to be congratulated on his "idealism." In reality you might just as well expect to be congratulated because, whenever you do a sum, you try to get it quite right. To be sure, perfect arithmetic is "an ideal"; you will certainly make some mistakes in some calculations. But there is nothing very fine about trying to be quite accurate at each step in each sum. It would be idiotic not to try; for every mistake is going to cause you trouble later on. In the same way every moral failure is going to cause trouble, probably to others and certainly to yourself. By talking about rules and obedience instead of "ideals" and "idealism," we help to remind ourselves of these facts.

Now let us go a step further. There are two ways in which the human machine goes wrong. One is when human individuals drift apart from one another, or else collide with one another and do one another damage, by cheating or bullying. The other is when things go wrong inside the individual—when the different parts of him (his different faculties, and desires, and so on) either drift apart or interfere with one another. You can get the idea plain if you think of us as a fleet of ships sailing in formation. The voyage will be a success only, in the first place, if the ships do not collide and get in one another's way; and, secondly, if each ship is seaworthy and has her engines in good order. As a matter of fact, you cannot have either of these two things without the other. If the ships keep on having collisions, they will not remain seaworthy very long. On the other hand, if their steering gears are out of order, they will not be able to avoid collisions. Or, if you like, think of humanity as a band playing a tune. To get a good result, you need two things. Each player's individual instrument must be in tune and also each must come in at the right moment so as to combine with all the others.

But there is one thing we have not yet taken into account. We have not asked where the fleet is trying to get to, or what piece of music the band is trying to play. The instruments might be all in tune and might all come in at the right moment, but even so the performance would not be a success if they had been engaged to provide dance music and actually played nothing but Dead Marches. And however well the fleet sailed, its voyage would be a failure it it were meant to reach New York and actually arrived at Calcutta.

Morality, then, seems to be concerned with three things. Firstly, with fair play and harmony between individuals. Secondly, with what might be called tidying up or harmonizing the things inside each individual. Thirdly, with the general purpose of human life as a whole: what man was made for: what course the whole fleet ought to be on: what tune the conductor of the band wants it to play.

The Tao

THE CHINESE . . . speak of a great thing (the greatest thing) called the *Tao*. It is the reality beyond all predicates, the abyss that was before the Creator Himself. It is Nature, it is the Way, the Road. It is the Way in which the universe goes on, the Way in which things everlastingly emerge, stilly and tranquilly, into space and time. It is also the Way which every man should tread in imitation of that cosmic and supercosmic progression, conforming all activities to that great exemplar. "In ritual," say the Analects, "it is harmony with Nature that is prized." The ancient Jews likewise praise the Law as being "true" (Psalm 119:151).

This conception in all its forms, Platonic, Aristotelian, Stoic, Christian, and Oriental alike, I shall henceforth refer to for brevity simply as "the *Tao*". . . . It is the doctrine of objective value, the belief that certain attitudes are really true, and others really false, to the kind of thing the universe is and the kind of things we are. Those who know the *Tao* can hold that to call children delightful or old men venerable is not simply to record a psychological fact about our own parental or filial emotions at the moment, but to recognize a quality which demands a certain response from us whether we make it or not. I myself do not enjoy the society of small children: because I speak from within the *Tao*, I recognize this as a defect in myself—just as a man may have to recognize that he is tone deaf or color blind. And because our approvals and disapprovals are thus recognitions of objective value or responses to an objective order, therefore emotional states can be in harmony with reasons (when we feel liking for what ought to be approved) or out of harmony with reason (when we perceive that liking is due but cannot feel it). No emotion is, in itself, a judgment: in that sense all emotions and sentiments are alogical. But they can be reasonable or unreasonable as they conform to Reason or fail to conform. The heart never takes the place of the head: but it can, and should, obey it. . . .

This thing which I have called for convenience the *Tao*, and which others may call Natural Law, or Traditional Morality, or the First Principles of Practical Reason, or the First Platitudes, is not one among a series of possible systems of value. It is the sole source of all value judgments. If it is rejected, all value is rejected. If any value is retained, it is retained. The effort to refute it and raise a new system of value in its place is self-contradictory. There never has been, and never will be, a radically new judgment of value in the history of the world. What purport to be new systems, or (as they now call them) "ideologies," all consist of fragments from the *Tao* itself, arbitrarily wrenched from their context in the whole and then swollen to madness in their isolation, yet still owing to the *Tao* and to it alone such validity as they possess. If my duty to my parents is a superstition, then so is my duty to posterity. If justice is a superstition, then so is my duty to my country or my race. If the pursuit of scientific knowledge is a real value, then so is conjugal fidelity. The rebellion of new ideologies against the *Tao* is a rebellion of the branches against the tree: if the rebels could succeed, they would find that they destroyed themselves. The human mind has no more power of inventing a new value than of imagining a new primary color, or, indeed, of creating a new sun and a new sky for it to move in.

Illustrations of the Tao

THE FOLLOWING ILLUSTRATIONS of the Natural Law are collected from such sources as come readily to the hand of one who is not a professional historian. The list makes no pretense of completeness. It will be noticed that writers . . . who wrote within the Christian tradition are quoted side by side with the New Testament. This would, of course, be absurd if I were trying to collect independent testimonies to the *Tao*. But (1) I am not trying to *prove* its validity by the argument from common consent. Its validity cannot be deduced. For those who do not perceive its rationality, even universal consent could not prove it. (2) The idea of collecting *independent* testimonies presupposes that "civilizations" have arisen in the world independently of one another; or even that humanity has had several independent emergences on this planet. The biology and anthropology involved in such an assumption are extremely doubtful. It is by no means certain that there has ever (in the sense required) been more than one civilization in all history. It is at least arguable that every civilization we find has been derived from another civilization and, in the last resort, from a single center—"carried" like an infectious disease or like the Apostolical succession.

I. THE LAW OF GENERAL BENEFICENCE

Negative

"I have not slain men." (Ancient Egyptian)

"Do not murder." (Ancient Jewish)

"Terrify not men or God will terrify thee." (Ancient Egyptian)

"In Nastrond (= Hell) I saw . . . murderers." (Old Norse)

"I have not brought misery upon my fellows. I have not made the beginning of every day laborious in the sight of him who worked for me." (Ancient Egyptian)

"I have not been grasping." (Ancient Egyptian)

"Who meditates oppression, his dwelling is overturned." (Babylonian)

"He who is cruel and calumnious has the character of a cat." (Hindu)

"Slander not." (Babylonian)

"Thou shalt not bear false witness against thy neighbor." (Ancient Jewish)

"Utter not a word by which anyone could be wounded." (Hindu)

"Has he . . . driven an honest man from his family? broken up a well cemented clan?" ' (Babylonian)

"I have not caused hunger. I have not caused weeping." (Ancient Egyptian)

"Never do to others what you would not like them to do to you." (Ancient Chinese)

"Thou shalt not hate thy brother in thy heart." (Ancient Jewish)

"He whose heart is in the smallest degree set upon goodness will dislike no one." (Ancient Chinese)

Positive

"Nature urges that a man should wish human society to exist and should wish to enter it." (Roman)

"By the fundamental Law of Nature Man [is] to be preserved as much as possible." (English: Locke)

"When the people have multiplied, what next should be done for them? The Master said, Enrich them. Jan Ch'iu said, When one has enriched them, what next should be done for them? The Master said, Instruct them." (Ancient Chinese)

"Speak kindness . . . show good will." (Babylonian)

"Men were brought into existence for the sake of men that they might do one another good." (Roman)

"Man is man's delight." (Old Norse)

"He who is asked for alms should always give." (Hindu)

"What good man regards any misfortune as no concern of his?" (Roman)

"I am a man: nothing human is alien to me." (Roman)

"Love thy neighbor as thyself." (Ancient Jewish)

"Love the stranger as thyself." (Ancient Jewish)

"Do to men what you wish men to do to you." (Christian)

II. THE LAW OF SPECIAL BENEFICENCE

"It is upon the trunk that a gentleman works. When that is firmly set up, the Way grows. And surely proper behavior to parents and elder brothers is the trunk of goodness." (Ancient Chinese)

"Brothers shall fight and be each others' bane." (Old Norse)

"Has he insulted his elder sister?" (Babylonian)

"You will see them take care of their kindred [and] the children of their friends . . . never reproaching them in the least." (American Indian)

"Love thy wife studiously. Gladden her heart all thy life long." (Ancient Egyptian)

"Nothing can ever change the claims of kinship for a right thinking man." (Anglo-Saxon)

"Did not Socrates love his own children, though he did so as a free man and as one not forgetting that the gods have the first claim on our friendship?" (Greek)

"Natural affection is a thing right and according to Nature." (Greek)

"I ought not to be unfeeling like a statue but should fulfill both my natural and artificial relations, as a worshipper, a son, a brother, a father, and a citizen." (Greek)

"This first I rede thee: be blameless to thy kindred. Take no vengeance even though they do thee wrong." (Old Norse)

"Is it only the sons of Atreus who love their wives? For every good man, who is right-minded, loves and cherishes his own." (Greek)

"The union and fellowship of men will be best reserved if each receives from us the more kindness in proportion as he is more closely connected with us." (Roman)

"Part of us is claimed by our country, part by our parents, part by our friends." (Roman)

"If a ruler . . . compassed the salvation of the whole state, surely you would call him Good? The Master said, It would no longer be a matter of 'Good.' He would without doubt be a Divine Sage." (Ancient Chinese)

"Has it escaped you that, in the eyes of gods and good men, your native land deserves from you more honor, worship, and reverence than your mother and father and all your ancestors? That you should give a softer answer to its anger than to a father's anger? That if you cannot persuade it to alter its mind you must obey it in all quietness, whether it binds you, or beats you, or sends you to a war where you may get wounds or death?" (Greek)

"If any provide not for his own, and specially for those of his own house, he hath denied the faith." (Christian)

"Put them in mind to obey magistrates." "I exhort that prayers be made for kings and all that are in authority." (Christian)

III. DUTIES TO PARENTS, ELDERS, ANCESTORS

"Your father is an image of the Lord of Creation, your mother is an image of the Earth. For him who fails to honor them, every work of piety is in vain. This is the first duty." (Hindu)

"Has he despised Father and Mother?" (Babylonian)

"I was a staff by my Father's side. . . . I went in and out at his command." (Ancient Egyptian)

"Honor thy Father and thy Mother."
(Ancient Jewish)

"To care for parents." (Greek)

"Children, old men, the poor, and the sick, should be considered as the lords of the atmosphere." (Hindu)

"Rise up before the hoary head and honor the old man." (Ancient Jewish)

"I tended the old man, I gave him my staff." (Ancient Egyptian)

"You will see them take care . . . of old men." (American Indian)

"I have not taken away the oblations of the blessed dead." (Ancient Egyptian)

"When proper respect toward the dead is shown at the end and continued after they are far away, the moral force of a people has reached its highest point." (Ancient Chinese)

IV. DUTIES TO CHILDREN AND POSTERITY

"Children, the old, the poor, etc., should be considered as lords of the atmosphere." (Hindu)

"To marry and to beget children." (Greek)

"Can you conceive an Epicurean commonwealth? . . . What will happen? Whence is the population to be kept up? Who will educate them? Who will be Director of Adolescents? Who will be Director of Physical Training? What will be taught?" (Greek)

"Nature produces a special love of offspring." "To live according to Nature is the supreme good." (Roman)

"The second of these achievements is no less glorious than the first; for while the first did good on one occasion, the second will continue to benefit the state forever." (Roman)

"Great reverence is owed to a child." (Ancient Chinese)

"The Master said, Respect the young." (Ancient Chinese)

"The killing of the women and more especially of the young boys and girls who are to go to make up the future strength of the people, is the saddest part . . . and we feel it very sorely." (American Indian)

V. THE LAW OF JUSTICE

Sexual Justice

"Has he approached his neighbor's wife?" (Babylonian)

"Thou shalt not commit adultery." (Ancient Jewish)

"I saw in Nastrond (= Hell) . . . beguilers of others' wives." (Old Norse)

Honesty

"Has he drawn false boundaries?" (Babylonian)

"To wrong, to rob, to cause to be robbed." (Babylonian)

"I have not stolen." (Ancient Egyptian)

"Thou shalt not steal." (Ancient Jewish)

"Choose loss rather than shameful gains." (Greek)

"Justice is the settled and permanent intention of rendering to each man his rights." (Roman)

"If the native made a 'find' of any kind (for example, a honey tree) and marked it, it was thereafter safe for him, as far as his own tribesmen were concerned, no matter how long he left it." (Australian Aborigines)

"The first point of justice is that none should do any mischief to another unless he has first been attacked by the other's wrongdoing. The second is that a man should treat common property as common property, and private property as his own. There is no such thing as private property by nature, but things have become private either through prior occupation (as when men of old came into empty territory) or by conquest, or law, or agreement, or stipulation, or casting lots." (Roman)

Justice in Court, etc.

"Who so takes no bribe . . . well pleasing is this to Samas." (Babylonian)

"I have not traduced the slave to him who is set over him." (Ancient Egyptian)

"Thou shalt not bear false witness against thy neighbor." (Ancient Jewish)

"Regard him whom thou knowest like him whom thou knowest not." (Ancient Egyptian)

"Do no unrighteousness in judgment. You must not consider the fact that one party is poor nor the fact that the other is a great man." (Ancient Jewish)

VI. THE LAW OF GOOD FAITH AND VERACITY

"A sacrifice is obliterated by a lie and the merit of alms by an act of fraud." (Hindu)

"Whose mouth, full of lying, avails not before thee: thou burnest their utterance." (Babylonian)

"With his mouth was he full of *Yea,* in his heart full of *Nay?*" (Babylonian)

"I have not spoken falsehood." (Ancient Egyptian)

"I sought no trickery, nor swore false oaths." (Anglo-Saxon)

"The Master said, Be of unwavering good faith." (Ancient Chinese)

"In Nastrond (= Hell) I saw the perjurers." (Old Norse)

"Hateful to me as are the gates of Hades is that man who says one thing, and hides another in his heart." (Greek)

"The foundation of justice is good faith." (Roman)

"[The Gentleman] must learn to be faithful to his superiors and to keep promises." (Ancient Chinese)

"Anything is better than treachery." (Old Norse)

VII. THE LAW OF MERCY

"The poor and the sick should be regarded as lords of the atmosphere." (Hindu)

"Who so makes intercession for the weak, well pleasing is this to Samas." (Babylonian)

"Has he failed to set a prisoner free?" (Babylonian)

"I have given bread to the hungry, water to the thirsty, clothes to the naked, a ferry boat to the boatless." (Ancient Egyptian)

"One should never strike a woman; not even with a flower." (Hindu)

"There, Thor, you got disgrace, when you beat women." (Old Norse)

"In the Dalebura tribe a woman, a cripple from birth, was carried about by the tribespeople in turn until her death at the age of sixty-six." "They never desert the sick." (Australian Aborigines)

"You will see them take care of . . . widows, orphans, and old men, never reproaching them." (American Indian)

"Nature confesses that she has given to the human race the tenderest hearts, by giving us the power to weep. This is the best part of us." (Roman)

"They said that he had been the mildest and gentlest of the kings of the world." (Anglo-Saxon)

"When thou cuttest down thine harvest . . . and hast forgot a sheaf . . . thou shalt not go again to fetch it: it shall be for the stranger, for the fatherless, and for the widow." (Ancient Jewish)

VIII. THE LAW OF MAGNANIMITY

A.

"There are two kinds of injustice: the first is found in those who do an injury, the second in those who fail to protect another from injury when they can." (Roman)

"Men always knew that when force and injury [were] offered they might be defenders of themselves; they knew that howsoever men may seek their own commodity, yet if this were done with injury unto others it was not to be suffered, but by all men and by all good means to be withstood." (English)

"To take no notice of a violent attack is to strengthen the heart of the enemy. Vigor is valiant, but cowardice is vile." (Ancient Egyptian)

"They came to the fields of joy, the fresh turf of the Fortunate Woods, and the dwellings of the Blessed . . . here was the company of those who had suffered wounds fighting for their fatherland." (Roman)

"Courage has got to be harder, heart the stouter, spirit the sterner, as our strength weakens. Here lies our lord, cut to pieces, our best man in the dust. If any-one thinks of leaving this battle, he can howl forever." (Anglo-Saxon)

"Praise and imitate that man to whom, while life is pleasing, death is not grievous." (Stoic)

"The Master said, Love learning and if attacked be ready to die for the Good Way." (Ancient Chinese)

B.

"Death is to be chosen before slavery and base deeds." (Roman)

"Death is better for every man than life with shame." (Anglo-Saxon)

"Nature and Reason command that nothing un-comely, nothing effeminate, nothing lascivious be done or thought." (Roman)

"We must not listen to those who advise us 'being men to think human thoughts, and being mortal to think mortal thoughts,' but must put on immortality as much as is possible and strain every nerve to live ac-cording to that best part of us, which, being small in bulk, yet much more in its power and honor surpasses all else." (Ancient Greek)

"The soul then ought to conduct the body, and the spirit of our minds the soul. This is therefore the first Law, whereby the highest power of the mind requireth obedience at the hands of all the rest." (English)

"Let him not desire to die, let him not desire to live, let him wait for his time . . . let him patiently bear hard words, entirely abstaining from bodily pleasures." (Ancient Indian)

"He who is unmoved, who has restrained his senses . . . is said to be devoted. As a flame in a windless place that flickers not, so is the devoted." (Ancient Indian)

C.

"Is not the love of Wisdom, a practice of death?" (Ancient Greek)

"I know that I hung on the gallows for nine nights, wounded with the spear as a sacrifice to Odin, myself offered to Myself." (Old Norse)

"Verily, verily I say to you unless a grain of wheat falls into the earth and dies, it remains alone, but if it dies it bears much fruit. He who loves his life loses it." (Christian)

Joy

IMAGINATION IS A VAGUE WORD and I must make some distinctions. It may mean the world of reverie, daydream, wish-fulfilling fantasy. . . . Invention is essentially different from reverie; if some fail to recognize the difference, that is because they have not themselves experienced both. . . . If we use the word imagination in a third sense, and the highest of all, this invented world was not imaginative. But certain other experiences were, and I will now try to record them. . . .

The first is itself the memory of a memory. As I stood beside a flowering currant bush on a summer day, there suddenly arose in me without warning, and as if from a depth not of years but of centuries, the memory of that earlier morning at the Old House when my brother had brought his toy garden into the nursery. It is difficult to find words strong enough for the sensation which came over me; Milton's "enormous bliss" of Eden (giving the full, ancient meaning to "enormous") comes somewhere near it. It was a sensation, of course, of desire; but desire for what? not, certainly, for a biscuit tin filled with moss, nor even (though that came into it) for my own past. . . . Before I knew what I desired, the desire itself was gone, the whole glimpse withdrawn, the world turned commonplace again, or only stirred by a longing for the longing that had just ceased. It had taken only a moment of time; and in a certain sense everything else that had ever happened to me was insignificant in comparison.

The second glimpse came through *Squirrel Nutkin;* through it only, though I loved all the Beatrix Potter books. But the rest of them were merely entertaining; it administered the shock, it was a trouble. It troubled me with what I can only describe as the Idea of Autumn. It sounds fantastic to say that one can be enamored of a season, but that is something like what happened; and, as before, the experience was one of intense desire. And one went back to the book, not to gratify the desire (that was impossible—how can one *possess* Autumn?) but to reawake it. And in this experience also there was the same surprise and the same sense of incalculable importance. It was something quite different from ordinary life and even from ordinary pleasure; something, as they would now say, "in another dimension."

The third glimpse came through poetry. I had become fond of Longfellow's *Saga of King Olaf:* fond of it in a casual, shallow way for its story and its vigorous rhythms. But then, and quite different from such pleasures, and like a voice from far more distant regions, there came a moment when I idly turned the pages of the book and found the unrhymed translation of *Tegner's Drapa* and read

> I heard a voice that cried,
> Balder the beautiful
> Is dead, is dead—

I knew nothing about Balder; but instantly I was uplifted into huge regions of northern sky, I desired with almost sickening intensity something never to be described (except that it is cold, spacious, severe, pale, and remote) and then, as in the other examples, found myself at the very same moment already falling out of that desire and wishing I were back in it.

The reader who finds these three episodes of no interest need read this book [*Surprised by Joy*] no further, for in a sense the central story of my life is about nothing else. For those who are still disposed to proceed, I will only underline the quality common to the three experiences; it is that of an unsatisfied desire which is itself more desirable than any other satisfaction. I call it Joy, which is here a technical term and must be sharply distinguished both from Happiness and from Pleasure. Joy (in my sense) has indeed one characteristic, and one only, in common with them; the fact that anyone who has experienced it will want it again. Apart from that, and considered only in its quality, it might almost equally well be called a particular kind of unhappiness or grief. But then it is a kind we want. I doubt whether anyone who has tasted it would ever, if both were in his power, exchange it for all the pleasures in the world. But then Joy is never in our power and pleasure often is. . . .

With my mother's death all settled happiness, all that was tranquil and reliable, disappeared from my life. There was to be much fun, many pleasures, many stabs of Joy; but no more of the old security. It was sea and islands now; the great continent had sunk like Atlantis. . . .

As for Joy, I labeled it "esthetic experience" and talked much about it under that name and said it was very "valuable." But it came very seldom and when it came it didn't amount to much. . . .

This discovery flashed a new light back on my whole life. I saw that all my waitings and watchings for Joy, all my vain hopes to find some mental content on which I could, so to speak, lay my finger and say, "This is it," had been a futile attempt to contemplate the enjoyed. All that such watching and waiting ever *could* find would be either an image (Asgard, the Western Garden, or what not) or a quiver in the diaphragm. I should never have to bother again about these images or sensations. I knew now that they were merely the mental track left by the passage of Joy—not the wave but the wave's imprint on the sand. The inherent dialectic of desire itself had in a way already shown me this; for all images and sensations, if idolatrously mistaken for Joy itself, soon honestly confessed themselves inadequate. All said, in the last resort, "It is not I. I am only a reminder. Look! Look! What do I remind you of?"

So far, so good. But it is at the next step that awe overtakes me. There was no doubt that Joy was a desire (and, insofar as it was also simultaneously a good, it was also a kind of love). But a desire is turned not to itself but to its object. Erotic love is not like desire for food, nay, a love for one woman differs from a love for another woman in the very same way and the very same degree as the two women differ from one another. Even our desire for one wine differs in tone from our desire for another. Our intellectual desire (curiosity) to know the true answer to a question is quite different from our desire to find that one answer, rather than another, is true. The form of the desired is in the desire. It is the object which makes the desire harsh or sweet, coarse or choice, "high" or "low." It is the object that makes the desire itself desirable or hateful. I perceived (and this was a wonder of wonders) that just as I had been wrong in supposing that I really desired the Garden of the Hesperides, so also I had been equally wrong in supposing that I desired Joy itself. Joy itself, considered simply as an event in my own mind, turned out to be of no value at all. All the value lay in that of which Joy was the desiring. And that object, quite clearly, was no state of my own mind or body at all. In a way, I had proved this by elimination. I had tried everything in my own mind and body; as it were, asking myself, "Is it this you want: Is it this?" Last of all I had asked if Joy itself was what I wanted; and, labeling it "esthetic experience," had pretended I could answer Yes. But that answer too had broken down. Inexorably Joy proclaimed, "You want—I myself am your want or—something other, outside, not you nor any state of you." I did not yet ask, Who is the desired? only What is it? But this brought me already into the region of awe, for thus I understood that in deepest solitude there is a road right out of the self, a commerce with something which, by refusing to identify itself with any object of the senses, or anything whereof we have biological or social need, or anything imagined, or any state of our own minds, proclaims itself sheerly objective. Far more objective than bodies, for it is not, like them, clothed in our senses; the naked Other, imageless (though our imagination salutes it with a hundred images), unknown, undefined, desired. . . .

It may be asked whether my terror was at all relieved by the thought that I was now approaching the source from which those arrows of Joy had been shot at me ever since childhood. Not in the least. No slightest hint was vouchsafed me that there ever had been or ever would be any connection between God and Joy. If anything, it was the reverse. I had hoped that the heart of reality might be of such a kind that we can best symbolize it as a place; instead, I found it to be a Person. For all I knew, the total rejection of what I called Joy might be one of the demands, might be the very first demand, He would make upon me. There was no strain of music from within, no smell of eternal orchids at the threshold, when I was dragged through the doorway. No kind of desire was present at all. . . .

But what, in conclusion, of Joy? For that, after all, is what the story has mainly been about. To tell you the truth, the subject has lost nearly all interest for me since I became a Christian.

Theology

EVERYONE HAS WARNED ME not to tell you what I am going to tell you. . . . They all say "the ordinary reader does not want Theology; give him plain practical religion." I have rejected their advice. I do not think the ordinary reader is such a fool. Theology means "the science of God," and I think any man who wants to think about God at all would like to have the clearest and most accurate ideas about Him which are available. You are not children: why should you be treated like children?

In a way I quite understand why some people are put off

by Theology. I remember once when I had been giving a talk to the R.A.F., an old, hard-bitten officer got up and said, "I've no use for all that stuff. But, mind you, I'm a religious man too. I *know* there's a God. I've *felt* Him: out alone in the desert at night: the tremendous mystery. And that's just why I don't believe all your neat little dogmas and formulas about Him. To anyone who's met the real thing they all seem so petty and pedantic and unreal!"

Now in a sense I quite agreed with that man. I think he had probably a real experience of God in the desert. And when he turned from that experience to the Christian creeds, I think he really was turning from something real, to something less real. In the same way, if a man has once looked at the Atlantic from the beach, and then goes and looks at a map of the Atlantic, he also will be turning from something real to something less real: turning from real waves to a bit of colored paper. But here comes the point. The map is admittedly only colored paper, but there are two things you have to remember about it. In the first place, it is based on what hundreds and thousands of people have found out by sailing the real Atlantic. In that way it has behind it masses of experience just as real as the one you could have from the beach; only, while yours would be a single isolated glimpse, the map fits all those different experiences together. In the second place, if you want to go anywhere, the map is absolutely necessary. As long as you are content with walks on the beach, your own glimpses are far more fun than looking at a map. But the map is going to be more use than walks on the beach if you want to get to America.

Now Theology is like the map. Merely learning and thinking about the Christian doctrines, if you stop there, is less real and less exciting than the sort of thing my friend got in the desert. Doctrines are not God: they are only a kind of map. But the map is based on the experience of hundreds of people who really were in touch with God—experiences compared with which any thrills or pious feelings you or I are likely to get on our own way are very elementary and very confused. And secondly, if you want to get any further, you must use the map. You see, what happened to that man in the desert may have been real, and was certainly exciting, but nothing comes of it. It leads nowhere. There is nothing to do about it. In fact, that is just why a vague religion—all about feeling God in nature, and so on—is so attractive. It is all thrills and no work; like watching the waves from the beach. But you will not get to Newfoundland by studying the Atlantic that way, and you will not get eternal life by simply feeling the presence of God in flowers or music. Neither will you get anywhere by looking at maps without going to sea. Nor will you be very safe if you go to sea without a map.

In other words, Theology is practical: especially now. In the old days, where there was less education and discussion, perhaps it was possible to get on with a very few simple ideas about God. But it is not so now. Everyone reads, everyone hears things discussed. Consequently if you do not listen to Theology, that will not mean that you have no ideas about God. It will mean that you have a lot of wrong ones—bad, muddled, out-of-date ideas. For a great many of the ideas about God which are trotted out as novelties today, are simply the ones which real Theologians tried centuries ago and rejected. To believe in the popular religion of modern England is retrogression—like believing the earth is flat.

For when you get down to it, is not the popular idea of Christianity simply this: that Jesus Christ was a great moral teacher and that if only we took his advice we might be able to establish a better social order and avoid another war? Now, mind you, that is quite true. But it tells you much less than the whole truth about Christianity and it has no practical importance at all.

It is quite true that if we took Christ's advice, we should

soon be living in a happier world. You need not even go as far as Christ. If we did all that Plato or Aristotle or Confucius told us, we should get on a great deal better than we do. And so what? We have never followed the advice of the great teachers. Why are we likely to begin now? Why are we more likely to follow Christ than any of the others? Because He is the best moral teacher? But that makes it even less likely that we shall follow Him. If we cannot take the elementary lessons, is it likely we are going to take the most advanced one: If Christianity only means one more bit of good advice, then Christianity is of no importance. There has been no lack of good advice for the last four thousand years. A bit more makes no difference.

But as soon as you look at any real Christian writings, you find that they are talking about something quite different from this popular religion. They say that Christ is the Son of God (whatever that means). They say that those who give Him their confidence can also become Sons of God (whatever that means). They say that His death saved us from our sins (whatever that means).

There is no good complaining that these statements are difficult. Christianity claims to be telling us about another world, about something behind the world we can touch and hear and see. You may think the claim false; but if it were true, what it tells us would be bound to be difficult—at least as difficult as modern Physics, and for the same reason.

Now the point in Christianity which gives us the greatest shock is the statement that by attaching to Christ we can "become Sons of God." One asks "Aren't we Sons of God already? Surely the fatherhood of God is one of the main Christian ideas?" Well, in a certain sense, no doubt we are sons of God already. I mean, God brought us into existence and loves us and looks after us, and in that way is like a father. But when the Bible talks of our "becoming" Sons of God, obviously it must mean something different. And that brings us up against the very center of Theology.

Divine Omnipotence

Omnipotence MEANS "power to do all, or everything." (The original meaning in Latin may have been "power *over* or *in* all." I give what I take to be current sense.) And we are told in Scripture that "with God all things are possible." It is common enough, in argument with an unbeliever, to be told that God, if He existed and were good, would do this or that; and then, if we point out that the proposed action is impossible, to be met with the retort, "But I thought God was supposed to be able to do anything." This raises the whole question of impossibility.

In ordinary usage the word *impossible* generally implies a suppressed clause beginning with the word *unless*. Thus it is impossible for me to see the street from where I sit writing at this moment; that is, it is impossible to see the street *unless* I go up to the top floor where I shall be high enough to overlook the intervening building. If I had broken my leg I should say "But it is impossible to go up to the top floor"—meaning, however, that it is impossible *unless* some friends turn up who will carry me. Now let us advance to a different plane of impossibility, by saying "It is, at any rate, impossible to see the street *so long as* I remain where I am and the intervening building remains where it is." Someone might add "unless the nature of space, or of vision, were different from what it is." I do not know what the best philosophers and scientists would say to this, but I should have to reply "I don't know whether space and vision *could possibly* have been of such a nature as you suggest." Now it is clear that the words *could possibly* refer to some absolute kind of possibility or impossibility which is different from the relative possibilities and impossibilities we have been considering. I cannot say whether seeing round corners is, in this new sense, possible or not, because I do not know whether it is self-contradictory or not. But I know very well that if it is self-contradictory it is absolutely impossible. The absolutely impossible may also be called the intrinsically impossible because it carries its impossibility within itself, instead of borrowing it from other impossibilities which in their turn depend upon others. It has no *unless* clause attached to it. It is impossible under all conditions, and in all worlds, and for all agents.

"All agents" here includes God Himself. His Omnipotence means power to do all that is intrinsically possible, not to do the intrinsically impossible. You may attribute miracles to Him, but not nonsense. This is no limit to His power. If you choose to say "God can give a creature free will and at the same time withhold free will from it," you have not succeeded in saying *anything* about God: meaningless combinations of words do not suddenly acquire meaning simply because we prefix to them the two other words "God can." It remains true that all *things* are possible with God: the intrinsic impossibilities are not things but nonentities. It is no more possible for God than for the weakest of His creatures to carry out both of two mutually exclusive alternatives; not because His power meets an obstacle, but because nonsense remains nonsense even when we talk it about God.

Divine Goodness

BY THE GOODNESS of God we mean nowadays almost exclusively His lovingness; and in this we may be right. And by Love, in this context, most of us mean kindness—the desire to see others than the self happy; not happy in this way or in that, but just happy. What would really satisfy us would be a God who said of anything we happened to like doing, "What does it matter so long as they are contented?" We want, in fact, not so much a Father in Heaven as a grandfather in heaven—a senile benevolence who, as they say, "liked to see young people enjoying themselves," and whose plan for the universe was simply that it might be truly said at the end of each day, "a good time was had by all." Not many people, I admit, would formulate a theology in precisely those terms: but a conception not very different lurks at the back of many minds. I do not claim to be an exception: I should very much like to live in a universe which was governed on such lines. But since it is abundantly clear that I don't, and since I have reason to believe, nevertheless, that God is Love, I conclude that my conception of love needs corrections.

I might, indeed, have learned, even from the poets, that Love is something more stern and splendid than mere kindness: that even the love between the sexes is, as in Dante, "a lord of terrible aspect." There is kindness in Love: but Love and kindness are not coterminous, and when kindness (in the sense given above) is separated from the other elements of Love, it involves a certain fundamental indifference to its object, and even something like contempt of it. Kindness consents very readily to the removal of its object—we have all met people whose kindness to animals is constantly leading them to kill animals lest they should suffer. Kindness, merely as such, cares not whether its object becomes good or bad, provided only that it escapes suffering. As Scripture points out, it is bastards who are spoiled: the legitimate sons, who are to carry on the family tradition, are punished (Hebrews 12:8). It is for people whom we care nothing about that we demand happiness on any terms: with our friends, our lovers, our children, we are exacting and would rather see them suffer much than be happy in contemptible and estranging modes. If God is Love, He is, by definition, something more than mere kindness. And it appears, from all records, that though He has often rebuked us and condemned us, He has never regarded us with contempt. He has paid us the intolerable compliment of loving us, in the deepest, most tragic, most inexorable sense.

Begetting and Making

ONE OF THE CREEDS says that Christ is the Son of God "begotten, not created"; and it adds "begotten by his Father before all worlds." Will you please get it quite clear that this has nothing to do with the fact that when Christ was born on earth as a man, that man was the son of a virgin? We are not now thinking about the Virgin Birth. We are thinking about something that happened before nature was created at all, before time began. "Before all worlds" Christ is begotten, not created. What does it mean?

We don't use the words *begetting* or *begotten* much in modern English, but everyone still knows what they mean. To beget is to become the father of: to create is to make. And the difference is this. When you beget, you beget something of the same kind as yourself. A man begets human babies, a beaver begets little beavers, and a bird begets eggs which turn into little birds. But when you make, you make something of a different kind from yourself. A bird makes a nest, a beaver builds a dam, a man makes a wireless set—or he may make something more like himself than a wireless set: say, a statue. If he is a clever enough carver, he may make a statue which is very like a man indeed. But, of course, it is not a real man; it only looks like one. It cannot breathe or think. It is not alive.

Now that is the first thing to get clear. What God begets is God; just as what man begets is man. What God creates is not God; just as what man makes is not man. That is why men are not Sons of God in the sense that Christ is. They may be like God in certain ways, but they are not things of the same kind. They are more like statues or pictures of God.

A statue has the shape of a man but it is not alive. In the same way, man has (in a sense I am going to explain) the "shape" or likeness of God, but he has not got the kind of life God has. Let us take the first point (man's resemblance to God) first. Everything God has made has some likeness to Himself. Space is like Him in its hugeness: not that the greatness of space is the same kind of greatness as God's but it is a sort of symbol of it, or a translation of it into nonspiritual terms. Matter is like God in having energy: though, again, of course, physical energy is a different kind of thing from the power of God. The vegetable world is like Him because it is alive, and He is the "living God." But life, in this biological sense, is not the same as the life there is in God: it is only a kind of symbol or shadow of it. When we come on to animals, we find other kinds of resemblance to the unceasing activity and the creativeness of God. In the higher mammals we get the beginnings of instinctive affection. That is not the same thing as the love that exists in God: but it is like it—rather in the way that a picture drawn on a flat piece of paper can nevertheless be "like" a landscape. When we come to man, the highest of the animals, we get the completest resemblance to God which we know of. (There may be creatures in other worlds who are more like God than man is, but we do not know about them.) Man not only lives, but loves and reasons: biological life reaches its highest known level in him.

But what man, in his natural condition, has not got, is Spiritual life—the higher and different sort of life that exists in God. We use the same word *life* for both: but if you thought that both must therefore be the same sort of thing, that would be like thinking that the "greatness" of space and the "greatness" of God were the same sort of greatness. In reality, the difference between Biological life and Spiritual life is so important that I am going to give them two distinct names. The Biological sort which comes to us through Nature, and which (like everything else in Nature) is always tending to run down and decay so that it can only be kept up by incessant subsidies from Nature in the form of air, water, food, etc., is *Bios*. The Spiritual life which is in God from all eternity, and which made the whole natural universe, is *Zoë*. *Bios* has, to be sure, a certain shadowy or symbolic resemblance to *Zoë*: but only the sort of resemblance there is between a photo and a place, or a statue and a man. A man who changed from having *Bios* to having *Zoë* would have gone through as big a change as a statue which changed from being a carved stone to being a real man.

And that is precisely what Christianity is about. This world is a great sculptor's shop. We are the statues and there is a rumor going round the shop that some of us are some day going to come to life.

Spirit, Spirits, Spiritual

WHEN DEVOTIONAL WRITERS talk of the "spiritual life"—and often when they talk of the "supernatural life" or when I myself . . . talked of *Zoë*—they mean this *absolutely* Supernatural life which no creature can be given simply by being created but which every rational creature can have by voluntarily surrendering itself to the life of Christ. But much confusion arises from the fact that in many books the words "Spirit" or "Spiritual" are also used to mean the *relatively* supernatural element in Man, the element external to *this* Nature which is (so to speak) "issued" or handed out to him by the mere fact of being created as a Man at all.

It will perhaps be helpful to make a list of the senses in which the words "spirit," "spirits," and "spiritual" are, or have been, used in English.

1. The chemical sense, e.g. "Spirits evaporate very quickly."

2. The (now obsolete) medical sense. The older doctors believed in certain extremely fine fluids in the human body which were called "the spirits." As medical science this view has long been abandoned, but it is the origin of some expressions we still use; as when we speak of being "in high spirits" or "in low spirits" or say that a horse is "spirited" or that a boy is "full of animal spirits."

3. "Spiritual" is often used to mean simply the opposite of "bodily" or "material." Thus all that is immaterial in man (emotions, passions, memory, etc.) is often called "spiritual." It is very important to remember that what is "spiritual" in this sense is not necessarily good. There is nothing especially fine about the mere fact of immateriality. Immaterial things may, like material things, be good or bad or indifferent.

4. Some people use "spirit" to mean that relatively supernatural element which is given to every man at his creation—the rational element. This is, I think, the most useful way of employing the word. Here again it is important to realize that what is "spiritual" is not necessarily good. A Spirit (in this sense) can be either the best or the worst of created things. It is because Man is (in this sense) a spiritual animal that he can become either a son of God or a devil.

5. Finally, Christian writers use "spirit" and "spiritual" to mean the life which arises in such rational beings when they voluntarily surrender to Divine grace and become sons

of the Heavenly Father in Christ. It is in this sense, and in this sense alone, that the "spiritual" is always good.

The Three-Personal God

IN SPACE you can move in three ways—to left or right, backward or forward, up or down. Every direction is either one of these three or a compromise between them. They are called the three Dimensions. Now notice this. If you are using only one dimension, you could draw only a straight line. If you are using two, you could draw a figure: say, a square. And a square is made up of four straight lines. Now a step further. If you have three dimensions, you can then build what we call a solid body: say, a cube—a thing like a [die] or a lump of sugar. And a cube is made up of six squares.

Do you see the point? A world of one dimension would be a straight line. In a two-dimensional world, you still get straight lines, but many lines make one figure. In a three-dimensional world, you still get figures but many figures make one solid body. In other words, as you advance to more real and more complicated levels, you do not leave behind you the things you found on the simpler levels: you still have them, but combined in new ways—in ways you could not imagine if you knew only the simpler levels.

Now the Christian account of God involves just the same principle. The human level is a simple and rather empty level. On the human level one person is one being, and any two persons are two separate beings—just as, in two dimensions (say on a flat sheet of paper) one square is one figure, and any two squares are two separate figures. On the Divine level you still find personalities; but up there you find them combined in new ways which we, who do not live on that level, cannot imagine. In God's dimension, so to speak, you find a being who is three Persons while remaining one Being, just as a cube is six squares while remaining one cube. Of course, we cannot fully conceive a Being like that: just as, if we were so made that we perceived only two dimensions in space, we could never properly imagine a cube. But we can get a sort of faint notion of it. And when we do, we are then, for the first time in our lives, getting some positive idea, however faint, of something superpersonal—something more than a person. It is something we could never have guessed, and yet, once we have been told, one almost feels one ought to have been able to guess it because it fits in so well with all the things we know already.

You may ask, "If we cannot imagine a three-personal Being, what is the good of talking about Him?" Well, there isn't any good talking about Him. The thing that matters is being actually drawn into that three-personal life, and that may begin any time—tonight, if you like.

What I mean is this. An ordinary simple Christian kneels down to say his prayers. He is trying to get in touch with God. But if he is a Christian he knows that what is prompting him to pray is also God: God, so to speak, inside him. But he also knows that all his real knowledge of God comes through Christ, the Man who was God—that Christ is standing beside him, helping him to pray, praying for him. You see what is happening. God is the thing to which he is praying—the goal he is trying to reach. God is also the thing inside him which is pushing him on—the motive power. God is also the road or bridge along which he is being pushed to that goal. So that the whole threefold life of the three-personal Being is actually going on in that ordinary little bedroom where an ordinary man is saying his prayers. The man is being caught up into the higher kind of life—what I call *Zoë* or spiritual life: he is being pulled into God, by God, while still remaining himself.

The Trinity

I BEGIN . . . by asking you to get a certain picture clear in your minds. Imagine two books lying on a table one on top of the other. Obviously the bottom book is keeping the other one up—supporting it. It is because of the underneath book that the top one is resting, say, two inches from the surface of the table instead of touching the table. Let us call the underneath book A and the top one B. The position of A is causing the position of B. That is clear? Now let us imagine—it could not really happen, of course, but it will do for an illustration—let us imagine that both books have been in that position forever and ever. In that case B's position would always have been resulting from A's position. But all the same, A's position would not have existed before B's position. In other words, the result does not come *after* the cause. Of course, results usually do: you eat the cucumber first and have the indigestion afterward. But it is not so with all causes, and results. You will see in a moment why I think this important.

I said . . . that God is a Being which contains three Persons while remaining one Being, just as a cube contains six squares while remaining one body. But as soon as I begin trying to explain how these Persons are connected, I have to use words which make it sound as if one of them was there before the others. The First Person is called the Father and the Second the Son. We say that the First begets or produces the Second; we call it *begetting*, not *making*, because what He produces is of the same kind as Himself. In that way the word Father is the only word to use. But unfortunately it suggests that He is there first—just as a human father exists before his son. But that is not so. There is no before and after about it. And that is why I have spent some time trying to make clear how one thing can be the source, or cause, or origin, of another without being there before it. The Son exists because the Father exists: but there never was a time before the Father produced the Son.

Perhaps the best way to think of it is this. I asked you now to imagine those two books, and probably most of you did. That is, you made an act of imagination and as a result you had a mental picture. Quite obviously your act of imagining was the cause and the mental picture the result. But that does not mean that you first did the imagining and then got the picture. The moment you did it, the picture was there. Your will was keeping the picture before you all the time. Yet that act of will and the picture began at exactly the same moment and ended at the same moment. If there were a Being who had always existed and had always been imagining one thing, his act would always have been producing a mental picture; but the picture would be just as eternal as the act.

In the same way we must think of the Son always, so to speak, streaming forth from the Father, like light from a lamp, or heat from a fire, or thoughts from a mind. He is the self-expression of the Father—what the Father has to say. And there never was a time when He was not saying it. But have you noticed what is happening? All these pictures of light or heat are making it sound as if the Father and Son were two things instead of two Persons. So that, after all, the New Testament picture of a Father and a Son turns out to be much more accurate than anything we try to substitute for it. That is what always happens when you go away from the words of the Bible. It is quite right to go away from them for a moment in order to make some special point clear. But you must always go back. Naturally God knows how to describe Himself much better than we know how to describe Him. He knows that Father and Son is more like the relation between the First and Second Persons than anything else we can think of. Much the most important thing to know is that it is a relation of love. The Father delights in His Son; the Son looks up to His Father. . . .

The union between the Father and Son is such a live concrete thing that this union itself is also a Person. I know this is almost inconceivable but look at it thus. You know that among human beings, when they get together in a family, or a club, or a trade union, people talk about the "spirit" of that family, or club, or trade union. They talk about its "spirit" because the individual members, when they are together, do really develop particular ways of talking and behaving which they would not have if they were apart. It is as if a sort of communal personality came into existence. Of course, it is not a real person: it is only rather like a person. But that is just one of the differences between God and us. What grows out of the joint life of the Father and Son is a real Person, is in fact the Third of the three Persons who are God.

This third Person is called, in technical language, the Holy Ghost or the "spirit" of God. Do not be worried or surprised if you find it (or Him) rather vaguer or more shadowy in your mind than the other two. I think there is a reason why that must be so. In the Christian life you are not usually looking *at* Him: He is always acting through you. If you think of the Father as something "out there," in front of you, and of the Son as someone standing at your side, helping you to pray, trying to turn you into another son, then you have to think of the third Person as something inside you, or behind you. Perhaps some people might find it easier to begin with the third Person and work backward. God is love, and that love works through men—especially through the whole community of Christians. But this spirit of love is, from all eternity, a love going on between the Father and Son.

The Fall of Man

ACCORDING TO [the doctrine of the Fall], man is now a horror to God and to himself and a creature ill-adapted to the universe not because God made him so but because he has made himself so by the abuse of his free will. To my mind this is the sole function of the doctrine. It exists to guard against two sub-Christian theories of the origin of evil—Monism, according to which God Himself, being "above good and evil," produces impartially the effects to which we give those two names, and Dualism, according to which God produces good, while some equal and independent Power produces evil. Against both these views Christianity asserts that God is good; that He made all things good and for the sake of their goodness; that one of the good things He made, namely, the free will of rational creatures, by its very nature included the possibility of evil; and that creatures, availing themselves of this possibility, have become evil. Now this function—which is the only one I allow to the doctrine of the Fall—must be distinguished from two other functions which it is sometimes, perhaps, represented as performing, but which I reject. In the first place, I do not think the doctrine answers the question "Was it better for God to create than not to create?" . . . Since I believe God to be good, I am sure that, if the question has a meaning, the answer must be Yes. But I doubt whether the question has any meaning: and even if it has, I am sure that the an-

swer cannot be attained by the sort of value judgments
which men can significantly make. In the second place, I do
not think the doctrine of the Fall can be used to show that it
is "just," in terms of retributive justice, to punish individuals for the faults of their remote ancestors. Some forms of
the doctrine seem to involve this; but I question whether
any of them, as understood by its exponents, really meant
it. The Fathers may sometimes say that we are punished for
Adam's sin: but they much more often say that *we* sinned
"in Adam." It may be impossible to find out what they
meant by this, or we may decide that what they meant was
erroneous. But I do not think we can dismiss their way of
talking as a mere "idiom." Wisely, or foolishly, they believed that we were *really*—and not simply by legal fiction—involved in Adam's action. The attempt to formulate
this belief by saying that we were "in" Adam in a physical
sense—Adam being the first vehicle of the "immortal germ
plasm"—may be unacceptable: but it is, of course, a further
question whether the belief itself is merely a confusion or a
real insight into spiritual realities beyond our normal grasp.
At the moment, however, this question does not arise; for,
as I have said, I have no intention of arguing that the descent to modern man of inabilities contracted by his remote
ancestors is a specimen of retributive justice. For me it is
rather a specimen of those things necessarily involved in
the creation of a stable world. . . . It would, no doubt, have
been possible for God to remove by miracle the results of
the first sin committed by a human being; but this would
not have been much good unless He was prepared to remove the results of the second sin, and of the third, and so
on forever. If the miracles ceased, then sooner or later we
might have reached our present lamentable situation: if
they did not, then a world, thus continually underpropped
and corrected by Divine interference, would have been a
world in which nothing important ever depended on

human choice, and in which choice itself would soon cease from the certainty that one of the apparent alternatives before you would lead to no results and was therefore not really an alternative.

The Incarnation

THE SON OF GOD became a man to enable men to become sons of God. We do not know—anyway, I do not know —how things would have worked if the human race had never rebelled against God and joined the enemy. Perhaps every man would have been "in Christ," would have shared the life of the Son of God, from the moment he was born. Perhaps the *Bios* or natural life would have been drawn up into the *Zoë*, the uncreated life, at once and as a matter of course. But that is guesswork. You and I are concerned with the way things work now.

And the present state of things is this. The two kinds of life are now not only different (they would always have been that) but actually opposed. The natural life in each of us is something self-centered, something that wants to be petted and admired, to take advantage of other lives, to exploit the whole universe. And especially it wants to be left to itself: to keep well away from anything better, or stronger, or higher than it, anything that might make it feel small. It is afraid of the light and air of the spiritual world, just as people who have been brought up to be dirty are afraid of a bath. And in a sense it is quite right. It knows that if the spiritual life gets hold of it, all its self-centeredness and self-will are going to be killed and it is ready to fight tooth and nail to avoid that.

Did you ever think, when you were a child, what fun it

would be if your toys could come to life? Well suppose you could really have brought them to life. Imagine turning a tin soldier into a real little man. It would involve turning the tin into flesh. And suppose the tin soldier did not like it. He is not interested in flesh; all he sees is that the tin is being spoiled. He thinks you are killing him. He will do everything he can do to prevent you. He will not be made into a man if he can help it.

What you would have done about that tin soldier I do not know. But what God did about us was this. The Second Person in God, the Son, became human Himself: was born into the world as an actual man—a real man of a particular height, with hair of a particular color, speaking a particular language, weighing so many stone. The Eternal Being, who knows everything and who created the whole universe, became not only a man but (before that) a baby, and before that a fetus inside a Woman's body. If you want to get the hang of it, think how you would like to become a slug or a crab.

The result of this was that you now had one man who really was what all men were intended to be: one man in whom created life, derived from his Mother, allowed itself to be completely and perfectly turned into the begotten life. The natural human creature in Him was taken up fully into the divine Son. Thus in one instance humanity had, so to speak, arrived: had passed into the life of Christ. And because the whole difficulty for us is that the natural life has to be, in a sense, "killed," He chose an earthly career which involved the killing of His human desires at every turn— poverty, misunderstanding from His own family, betrayal by one of His intimate friends, being jeered at and manhandled by the Police, and execution by torture. And then, after being thus killed—killed every day in a sense—the human creature in Him, because it was united to the divine Son, came to life again. The Man in Christ rose again: not only the God. That is the whole point. For the first time we

saw a real man. One tin soldier—real tin, just like the rest—
had come fully and splendidly alive.

✷

One must be careful not to put this in a way which would
blur the distinction between the creation of a man and the
Incarnation of God. Could one, as a mere model, put it
thus? In creation God makes—invents—a person and "utters"—injects—him into the realm of Nature. In the Incarnation, God the Son takes the body and human soul of
Jesus, and, through that, the whole environment of Nature,
all the creaturely predicament, into His own being. So that
"He came down from Heaven" can almost be transposed
into "Heaven drew earth up into it," and locality, limita-
tion, sleep, sweat, footsore weariness, frustration, pain,
doubt, and death, are, from before all worlds, known by
God from within. The pure light walks the earth; the darkness, received into the heart of the Deity, is there swallowed up. Where, except in uncreated light, can the darkness be drowned?

✷

The central miracle asserted by Christians is the Incarnation. They say God became Man. Every other miracle pre-
pares for this, or exhibits this, or results from this. Just as
every natural event is the manifestation at a particular place
and moment of Nature's total character, so every particular
Christian miracle manifests at a particular place and moment the character and significance of the Incarnation.
There is no question in Christianity of arbitrary interfer-
ences just scattered about. It relates not a series of discon-
nected raids on Nature but the various steps of a stra-
tegically coherent invasion—an invasion which intends
complete conquest and "occupation." The fitness, and
therefore the credibility, of the particular miracles depends

on their relation to the Grand Miracle; all discussion of them in isolation from it is futile.

The fitness or credibility of the Grand Miracle itself cannot, obviously, be judged by the same standard. And let us admit at once that it is very difficult to find a standard by which it can be judged. If the thing happened, it was the central event in the history of the Earth—the very thing that the whole story has been about. Since it happened only once, it is by Hume's standards infinitely improbable. But then the whole history of the Earth has also happened only once; is it therefore incredible? Hence the difficulty, which weighs upon Christian and atheist alike, of estimating the probability of the Incarnation. It is like asking whether the existence of Nature herself is intrinsically probable. That is why it is easier to argue, on historical grounds, that the Incarnation actually occurred than to show, on philosophical grounds, the probability of its occurrence. The historical difficulty of giving for the life, sayings, and influence of Jesus any explanation that is not harder than the Christian explanation is very great. The discrepancy between the depth and sanity and (let me add) *shrewdness* of His moral teaching and the rampant megalomania which must lie behind His theological teaching unless He is indeed God, has never been satisfactorily got over. Hence the non-Christian hypotheses succeed one another with the restless fertility of bewilderment. Today we are asked to regard all the theological elements as later accretions to the story of a "historical" and merely human Jesus: yesterday we were asked to believe that the whole thing began with vegetation myths and mystery religions and that the pseudohistorical Man was only fadged up at a later date. . . .

Since the Incarnation, if it is a fact, holds this central position, and since we are assuming that we do not yet know it to have happened on historical grounds, we are in a position which may be illustrated by the following analogy.

Let us suppose we possess parts of a novel or a symphony. Someone now brings us a newly discovered piece of manuscript and says, "This is the missing part of the work. This is the chapter on which the whole plot of the novel really turned. This is the main theme of the symphony." Our business would be to see whether the new passage, if admitted to the central place which the discoverer claimed for it, did actually illuminate all the parts we had already seen and "pull them together." Nor should we be likely to go very far wrong. The new passage, if spurious, however attractive it looked at the first glance, would become harder and harder to reconcile with the rest of the work the longer we considered the matter. But if it were genuine, then at every fresh hearing of the music or every fresh reading of the book, we should find it settling down, making itself more at home, and eliciting significance from all sorts of details in the whole work which we had hitherto neglected. Even though the new central chapter or main theme contained great difficulties in itself, we should still think it genuine provided that it continually removed difficulties elsewhere. Something like this we must do with the doctrine of the Incarnation. Here, instead of a symphony or a novel, we have the whole mass of our knowledge. The credibility will depend on the extent to which the doctrine, if accepted, can illuminate and integrate that whole mass. It is much less important that the doctrine itself should be fully comprehensible. We believe that the sun is in the sky at midday in summer not because we can clearly see the sun (in fact, we cannot) but because we can see everything else. . . .

In the Christian story God descends to reascend. He comes down; down from the heights of absolute being into time and space, down into humanity; down further still, if embryologists are right, to recapitulate in the womb ancient and prehuman phases of life; down to the very roots and seabed of the Nature He had created. But he goes down to come up again and bring the whole ruined world up with

Him. One has the picture of a strong man stooping lower and lower to get himself underneath some great complicated burden. He must stoop in order to lift, he must almost disappear under the load before he incredibly straightens his back and marches off with the whole mass swaying on his shoulders. Or one may think of a diver, first reducing himself to nakedness, then glancing in midair, then gone with a splash, vanished, rushing down through green and warm water into black and cold water, down through increasing pressure into the deathlike region of ooze and slime and old decay; then up again, back to color and light, his lungs almost bursting, till suddenly he breaks surface again, holding in his hand the dripping, precious thing that he went down to recover. He and it are both colored now that they have come up into the light: down below, where it lay colorless in the dark, he lost his color too.

In this descent and reascent everyone will recognize a familiar pattern: a thing written all over the world. It is the pattern of all vegetable life. It must belittle itself into something hard, small, and deathlike, it must fall into the ground: thence the new life reascends. It is the pattern of all animal generation too. There is descent from the full and perfect organisms into the spermatozoon and ovum, and in the dark womb a life at first inferior in kind to that of the species which is being reproduced: then the slow ascent to the perfect embryo, to the living, conscious baby, and finally to the adult. So it is also in our moral and emotional life. The first innocent and spontaneous desires have to submit to the deathlike process of control or total denial: but from that there is a reascent to fully formed character in which the strength of the original material all operates but in a new way. Death and Rebirth—go down to go up—it is a key principle. Through this bottleneck, this belittlement, the highroad nearly always lies.

The Virgin Birth

THE VIRGIN BIRTH is a doctrine plainly stated in the Apostles' Creed that Jesus had no physical father, and was not conceived as a result of sexual intercourse. It is not a doctrine on which there is any dispute between Presbyterians as such and Episcopalians as such. A few individual Modernists in both these churches have abandoned it; but Presbyterianism or Episcopalianism in general and in actual historical instances through the centuries both affirm it. The exact details of such a miracle—an exact point at which a supernatural enters this world (whether by the creation of a new spermatozoon, or the fertilization of an ovum without a spermatozoon, or the development of a fetus without an ovum) are not part of the doctrine. These are matters in which no one is obliged and everyone is free, to speculate.

✳

I can understand the man who denies miracles altogether: but what is one to make of people who will believe other miracles and "draw the line" at the Virgin Birth? Is it that for all their lip service to the laws of Nature there is only one natural process in which they really believe? Or is it that they think they see in this miracle a slur upon sexual intercourse (though they might just as well see in the feeding of the five thousand an insult to bakers) and that sexual intercourse is the one thing still venerated in this unvenerating age? In reality the Miracle is no less, and no more, surprising than any others.

Perhaps the best way to approach it is from the remark I saw in one of the most archaic of our anti-God papers. The remark was that Christians believed in a God who had "committed adultery with the wife of a Jewish carpenter." The writer was probably merely "letting off steam" and did not really think that God, in the Christian story, had assumed human form and lain with a mortal woman, as Zeus lay with Alcmena. But if one had to answer this person, one would have to say that if you called the miraculous conception divine adultery, you would be driven to find a similar adultery in the conception of every child—nay, of every animal too. I am sorry to use the expression which will offend pious ears, but I do not know how else to make my point.

In a normal act of generation the father has no creative function. A microscopic particle of matter from his body, and a microscopic particle from the woman's body, meet. And with that there passes the color of his hair, and the hanging lower lip of her grandfather, and the form of humanity in all its complexity of bones, sinews, nerves, liver, and heart, and the form of those prehuman organisms which the embryo will recapitulate in the womb. Behind every spermatozoon lies the whole history of the universe: locked within it lies no inconsiderable part of the world's future. The weight or drive behind it is the momentum of the whole interlocked event which we call Nature up-to-date. And we know now that the "laws of Nature" cannot supply that momentum. If we believe that God created Nature, that momentum comes from Him. The human father is merely an instrument, a carrier, often an unwilling carrier, always simply the last in a long line of carriers—a line that stretches back far beyond his ancestors into prehuman and preorganic deserts of time, back to the creation of matter itself. That line is in God's hand. It is the instrument by which He normally creates a man. For He is the reality behind both Genius and Venus; no woman ever conceived a child, no mare a foal, without Him. But once, and for a special purpose, He dispensed with that long line which is

His instrument: once His life-giving finger touched a woman without passing through the ages of interlocked events. Once the great glove of Nature was taken off His hand. His naked hand touched her. There was, of course, a unique reason for it. That time He was creating not simply a man but the Man who was to be Himself: was creating Man anew: was beginning, at this divine and human point, the New Creation of all things. The whole soiled and weary universe quivered at this direct injection of essential life— direct, uncontaminated, not drained through all the crowded history of Nature. But it would be out of place here to explore the religious significance of the miracle. We are here concerned with it simply as Miracle—that and nothing more. As far as concerns the creation of Christ's human nature (the Grand Miracle whereby His divine nature enters into it is another matter), the miraculous conception is one more witness that here is Nature's Lord. He is doing now, small and close, what He does in a different fashion for every woman who conceives. He does it this time without a line of human ancestors: but even where He uses human ancestors, it is not the less He who gives life (Matthew 23:9). The bed is barren where that great third party, Genius, is not present.

Miracles of Fertility

THE EARLIEST of these was the conversion of water into wine at the wedding feast in Cana. This miracle proclaims that the God of all wine is present. The vine is one of the blessings sent by Jahweh: He is the reality behind the false god Bacchus. Every year, as part of the Natural order, God makes wine. He does so by creating a vegetable organism that can turn water, soil, and sunlight into a juice which will, under proper conditions, become wine. Thus, in a certain sense, He constantly turns water into wine, for wine, like all drinks, is but water modified. Once, and in one year only, God, now incarnate, short-circuits the process: makes wine in a moment: uses earthenware jars instead of vegetable fibers to hold the water. But uses them to do what He is always doing. The Miracle consists in the shortcut; but the event to which it leads is the usual one. If the thing happened, then we know that what has come into Nature is no anti-Natural spirit, no God who loves tragedy, and tears, and fasting *for their own sake* (however He may permit or demand them for special purposes) but the God of Israel who has through all these centuries given us wine to gladden the heart of man.

Other miracles that fall in this class are the two instances of miraculous feeding. They involve the multiplication of a little bread and a little fish into much bread and much fish. Once in the desert Satan had tempted Him to make bread of stones: He refused the suggestion. "The Son does nothing except what He sees the Father do"; perhaps one may without boldness surmise that the direct change from stone to bread appeared to the Son to be not quite in the hereditary style. Little bread into much bread is quite a different matter. Every year God makes a little corn into much corn: the seed is sown and there is an increase. And men say, according to their several fashions, "It is the laws of Nature," or, "It is Ceres, it is Adonis, it is the Corn King." But the laws of Nature are only a pattern: nothing will come to them unless they can, so to speak, take over the universe as a going concern. And as for Adonis, no man can tell us where he died or when he rose again. Here, at the feeding of the five thousand, is He whom we have ignorantly worshipped: the *real* Corn King who will die once and rise once at Jerusalem during the term of office of Pontius Pilate.

That same day He also multiplied fish. Look down into

every bay and almost every river. This swarming, undulating fecundity shows He is still at work "thronging the seas with spawn innumerable." The ancients had a god called Genius; the god of animal and human fertility, the patron of gynecology, embryology, and the marriage bed—the "genial" bed as they called it after its god Genius. But Genius is only another mask for the God of Israel, for it was He who at the beginning commanded all species "to be fruitful and multiply and replenish the earth." And now, that day, at the feeding of the thousands, incarnate God does the same: does close and small, under His human hands, a workman's hands, what he has always been doing in the seas, the lakes, and the little brooks.

Miracles of Healing

THE MIRACLES OF *Healing* . . . are now in a peculiar position. Men are ready to admit that many of them happened but are inclined to deny that they were miraculous. The symptoms of very many diseases can be aped by hysteria, and hysteria can often be cured by "suggestion." It could, no doubt, be argued that such suggestion is a spiritual power, and therefore (if you like) a supernatural power, and that all instances of "faith healing" are therefore Miracles. But in our terminology they would be miraculous only in the same sense in which every instance of human reason is miraculous: and what we are now looking for is miracles other than that. My own view is that it would be unreasonable to ask a person who has not yet embraced Christianity in its entirety to allow that all the healings mentioned in the Gospels were miracles—that is, that they go beyond the possibilities of human "suggestion." It is for the doctors to decide as regards each particular case—supposing that the narratives are sufficiently detailed to allow even probable diagnosis. . . . So far from belief in miracles depending upon ignorance of natural law, we are here finding for ourselves that ignorance of law which makes miracles unascertainable.

Without deciding in detail which of the healings must (apart from acceptance of the Christian faith) be regarded as miraculous, we can, however, indicate the kind of miracle involved. Its character can easily be obscured by the somewhat magical view which many people still take of ordinary and medical healing. There is a sense in which no doctor ever heals. The doctors themselves would be the first to admit this. The magic is not in the medicine but in the patient's body—in the *vis medicatrix naturae*, the recuperative or self-corrective energy of Nature. What the treatment does is to stimulate Natural functions or to remove what hinders them. We speak for convenience of the doctor, or the dressing, healing a cut. But in another sense every cut heals itself: no cut can be healed in a corpse. That same mysterious force which we call gravitational when it steers the planets and biochemical when it heals a live body, is the efficient cause of all recoveries. And that energy proceeds from God in the first instance. All who are cured are cured by Him, not merely in the sense that His providence provides them with medical assistance and wholesome environments, but also in the sense that their very tissues are repaired by the far-descended energy which, flowing from Him, energizes the whole system of Nature. But once He did it visibly to the sick in Palestine, a Man meeting with men. What in its general operations we refer to laws of Nature or once referred to Apollo or Asclepius thus reveals itself. The Power that always was behind all healings puts on a face and hands. Hence, of course, the apparent chanciness of the miracles. It is idle to complain that He heals those whom He happens to meet, not those whom He doesn't. To

be a man means to be in one place and not in another. The
world which would not know Him as present everywhere
was saved by His becoming *local*.

Miracles of Destruction

CHRIST'S SINGLE MIRACLE of Destruction, the withering of
the fig tree, has proved troublesome to some people, but I
think its significance is plain enough. The miracle is an
acted parable, a symbol of God's sentence on all that is
"fruitless" and specially, no doubt, on the official Judaism
of that age. That is its moral significance. As a miracle, it
again does in focus, repeats small and close, what God does
constantly and throughout Nature. We have seen . . . how
God, twisting Satan's weapon out of his hand, had become,
since the Fall, the God even of human death. But much
more, and perhaps ever since the creation, He has been the
God of the death of organisms. In both cases, though in
somewhat different ways, He is the God of death because
He is the God of Life: the God of human death because
through it increase of life now comes—the God of merely
organic death because death is part of the very mode by
which organic life spreads itself out in Time and yet remains new. A forest a thousand years deep is still collec-
tively alive because some trees are dying and others are
growing up. His human face, turned with negation in its
eyes upon that one fig tree, did once what His unincarnate
action does to all trees. No tree died that year in Palestine,
or any year anywhere, except because God did—or rather
ceased to do—something to it.

Miracle of the Resurrection

IN THE EARLIEST DAYS of Christianity an "apostle" was first and foremost a man who claimed to be an eyewitness of the Resurrection. Only a few days after the Crucifixion when two candidates were nominated for the vacancy created by the treachery of Judas, their qualification was that they had known Jesus personally both before and after His death and could offer firsthand evidence of the Resurrection in addressing the outer world (Acts 1:22). A few days later St. Peter, preaching the first Christian sermon, makes the same claim—"God raised Jesus, of which we all (we Christians) are witnesses" (Acts 2:32). In the first Letter to the Corinthians St. Paul bases his claim to apostleship on the same ground—"Am I not an apostle? Have I not seen the Lord Jesus?"

As this qualification suggests, to preach Christianity meant primarily to preach the Resurrection. Thus people who had heard only fragments of St. Paul's teaching at Athens got the impression that he was talking about two new gods, Jesus and Anastasis (that is, Resurrection) (Acts 17:18). The Resurrection is the central theme in every Christian sermon reported in the Acts. The Resurrection, and its consequences, were the "gospel" or good news which the Christians brought: what we call the "gospels," the narratives of Our Lord's life and death, were composed later for the benefit of those who had already accepted the *gospel*. They were in no sense the basis of Christianity: they were written for those already converted. The miracle of the Resurrection, and the theology of that miracle, comes first: the biography comes later as a comment on it. Nothing could be more unhistorical than to pick out selected sayings of Christ from the gospels and to regard those as the datum and the rest of the New Testament as a construction upon it. The first fact in the history of Christendom is a number of people who say they have seen the Resurrection. If they had died without making anyone else believe this "gospel," no gospels would ever have been written.

It is very important to be clear about what these people mean. When modern writers talk of the Resurrection, they usually mean one particular moment—the discovery of the Empty Tomb and the appearance of Jesus a few yards away from it. The story of that moment is what Christian apologists now chiefly try to support and skeptics chiefly try to impugn. But this almost exclusive concentration on the first five minutes or so of the Resurrection would have astonished the earliest Christian teachers. In claiming to have seen the Resurrection they were not necessarily claiming to have seen *that*. Some of them had, some of them had not. It had no more importance than any of the other appearances of the risen Jesus—apart from the poetic and dramatic importance which the beginnings of things must always have. What they were claiming was that they had all, at one time or another, met Jesus during the six or seven weeks that followed His death. Sometimes they seem to have been alone when they did so, but on one occasion twelve of them saw Him together, and on another occasion about five hundred of them. St. Paul says that the majority of the five hundred were still alive when he wrote the First Letter to the Corinthians, that is in about 55 A.D.

The "Resurrection" to which they bore witness was, in fact, not the action of rising from the dead but the state of having risen: a state, as they held, attested by intermittent meetings during a limited period (except for the special, and in some ways different, meeting vouchsafed to St. Paul). This termination of the period is important, for, as we shall see, there is no possibility of isolating the doctrine of the Resurrection from that of the Ascension.

The next point to notice is that the Resurrection was not regarded simply or chiefly as evidence for the immortality of the soul. It is, of course, often so regarded today: I have heard a man maintain that "the importance of the Resurrection is that it proves *survival*." Such a view cannot at any point be reconciled with the language of the New Testament. On such a view Christ would simply have done what all men do when they die: the only novelty would have been that in His case we were allowed to see it happening. But there is not in Scripture the faintest suggestion that the Resurrection was new evidence for something that had *in fact* been always happening. The New Testament writers speak as if Christ's achievement in rising from the dead was the first event of its kind in the whole history of the universe. He is the "first fruits," the "pioneer of life." He has forced open a door that has been locked since the death of the first man. He has met, fought, and beaten the King of Death. Everything is different because He has done so. This is the beginning of the New Creation: a new chapter in cosmic history has opened.

Miracle of the Walking on the Water

IN THE WALKING ON THE WATER we see the relations of spirit and Nature so altered that Nature can be made to do whatever spirit pleases. This new obedience of Nature is, of course, not to be separated even in thought from spirit's own obedience to the Father of Spirits. Apart from that proviso such obedience by Nature, if it were possible, would result in chaos: the evil dream of Magic arises from finite spirit's longing to get that power without paying that price. The evil reality of lawless applied science (which is Magic's son and heir) is actually reducing large tracts of Nature to disorder and sterility at this very moment. I do not know how radically Nature herself would need to be altered to make her thus obedient to spirits, which spirits have become wholly obedient to their source. One thing, at least, we must observe. If we are in fact spirits, not Nature's offspring, then there must be some point (probably the brain) at which created spirit even now can produce effects on matter not by manipulation or technics but simply by the wish to do so. If that is what you mean by Magic, then Magic is a reality manifested every time you move your hand or think a thought. And Nature, as we have seen, is not destroyed but rather perfected by her servitude.

Miracle of the Raising of Lazarus

THE RAISING OF LAZARUS differs from the Resurrection of Christ Himself because Lazarus, so far as we know, was not raised to a new and more glorious mode of existence but merely restored to the sort of life he had had before. The fitness of the miracle lies in the fact that He who will raise all men at the general resurrection here does it small and close, and in an inferior—merely anticipatory—fashion. For the mere restoration of Lazarus is as inferior in splendor to the *glorious* resurrection of the New Humanity as stone jars are to the green and growing vine or five little barley loaves to all the waving bronze and gold of a fat valley ripe for harvest. The resuscitation of Lazarus, so far as we can see, is simple reversal: a series of changes working in the direction opposite to that we have always experienced. At death, matter which has been organic begins to flow away into the inorganic, to be finally scattered and used (some of it) by other organisms. The resurrection of Lazarus involves the reverse process. The general resurrection involves the reverse process universalized—a rush of matter toward organization at the call of spirits which require it. It is presumably a foolish fancy (not justified by the words of Scripture) that each spirit should recover those particular units of matter which he ruled before. For one thing, they would not be enough to go round: we all live in secondhand suits and there are doubtless atoms in my chin which have served many another man, many a dog, many an eel, many a dinosaur. Nor does the unity of our bodies, even in this present life, consist in retaining the same particles. My form remains one, though the matter in it changes continually. I am, in that respect, like a curve in a waterfall.

Miracle of the Transfiguration

THE TRANSFIGURATION or "Metamorphosis" of Jesus is . . . , no doubt, an anticipatory glimpse of something to come. He is seen conversing with two of the ancient dead. The change which His own human form had undergone is described as one to luminosity, to "shining whiteness." A similar whiteness characterizes His appearances at the beginning of the book of Revelation. One rather curious detail is that this shining or whiteness affected His clothes as much as His body. St. Mark indeed mentions the clothes more explicitly than the face, and adds, with his inimitable naivety, that "no laundry could do anything like it." Taken by itself this episode bears all the marks of a "vision"; that is, of an experience which, though it may be divinely sent and may reveal great truth, yet is not, objectively speaking, the experience it seems to be. But if the theory of "vision" (or holy hallucination) will not cover the Resurrection appearances, it would be only a multiplying of hypotheses to introduce it here. We do not know to what phase or feature of the New Creation this episode points. It may reveal some special glorifying of Chirst's manhood at some phase of its history (since history it apparently has), or it may reveal the glory which that manhood always has in its New Creation: it may even reveal a glory which all risen men will inherit. We do not know.

Miracle of the Ascension

WE FEEL SURE that the [New Testament writers] thought they had seen their Master setting off on a journey for a "local" Heaven where God sat in a throne and where there was another throne waiting for Him. And I believe that, for this reason, whatever they had actually seen (sense perception, almost by hypothesis, would be confused at such a moment), they would almost certainly have remembered it as a vertical movement. What we must not say is that they "mistook" local "Heavens," and celestial throne rooms, and the like for the "spiritual" Heaven of union with God and supreme power and beatitude. You and I have been gradually disentangling different senses of the word Heaven. . . . It may be convenient here to make a list. Heaven can mean (1) The unconditioned Divine Life beyond all worlds. (2) Blessed participation in that Life by a created spirit. (3) The Whole Nature or system of conditions in which redeemed human spirits, still remaining human, can enjoy such participation fully and forever. This is the Heaven Christ goes to "prepare" for us. (4) The physical Heaven, the sky, the space in which Earth moves. What enables us to distinguish these senses and hold them clearly apart is not any special spiritual purity but the fact that we are the heirs to centuries of logical analysis: not that we are sons to Abraham but that we are sons to Aristotle. We are not to suppose that the writers of the New Testament mistook Heaven in sense four or three for Heaven in sense two or one. You cannot mistake a half sovereign for a sixpence until you know the English system of coinage—that is, until you know the difference between them. In their idea of Heaven all these meanings were latent, ready to be brought out by later analysis. They never thought merely of the blue sky or merely of a "spiritual" heaven. When they looked up at the blue sky, they never doubted that He was "ascending" in what we should call a "spiritual" sense. . . . A man who really believes that "Heaven" is in the sky may well, in his heart, have a far truer and more spiritual conception of it than many a modern logician who could expose that fallacy with a few strokes of his pen. For he who does the will of the Father shall know the doctrine. Irrelevant material splendors in such a man's idea of the vision of God will do no harm, for they are not there for their own sakes.

On Seeing a Miracle

YOU ARE PROBABLY QUITE RIGHT in thinking that you will never see a miracle done: you are probably equally right in thinking that there was a natural explanation of anything in your past life which seemed, at the first glance, to be "rum" or "odd." God does not shake miracles into Nature at random as if from a pepper-caster. They come on great occasions: they are found at the great ganglions of history—not of political or social history, but of that spiritual history which cannot be fully known by men. If your own life does not happen to be near one of those great ganglions, how should you expect to see one? If we were heroic missionaries, apostles, or martyrs, it would be a different matter. But why you or I? Unless you live near a railway, you will not see trains go past your windows. How likely is it that you or I will be present when a peace treaty is signed, when a great scientific discovery is made, when a dictator commits suicide? That we should see a miracle is even less likely. Nor, if we understand, shall we be anxious to do so. "Nothing almost sees miracles but misery." Miracles and martyrdoms tend to bunch about the same areas of history—areas we have naturally no wish to frequent. Do not, I earnestly advise you, demand an ocular proof unless you are already perfectly certain that it is not forthcoming.

The Second Coming

In *King Lear* (III:vii) there is a man who is such a minor character that Shakespeare has not given him even a name: he is merely "First Servant." All the characters around him—Regan, Cornwall, and Edmund—have fine long-term plans. They think they know how the story is going to end, and they are quite wrong. The servant has no such delusions. He has no notion how the play is going to go. But he understands the present scene. He sees an abomination (the blinding of old Gloucester) taking place. He will not stand it. His sword is out and pointed at his master's breast in a moment: then Regan stabs him dead from behind. That is his whole part: eight lines all told. But if it were real life and not a play, that is the part it would be best to have acted.

The doctrine of the Second Coming teaches us that we do not and cannot know when the world drama will end. The curtain may be rung down at any moment: say, before you have finished reading this paragraph. This seems to some people intolerably frustrating. So many things would be interrupted. Perhaps you were going to get married next month, perhaps you were going to get a raise next week: you may be on the verge of a great scientific discovery; you may be maturing great social and political reforms. Surely no good and wise God would be so very unreasonable as to cut all this short? Not *now,* of all moments!

But we think thus because we keep on assuming that we know the play. We do not know the play. We do not even know whether we are in Act I or Act V. We do not know who are the major and the minor characters. The Author knows. The audience, if there is an audience (if angels and archangels and all the company of Heaven fill the pit and the stalls), may have an inkling. But we, never seeing the play from outside, never meeting any characters except the tiny minority who are "on" in the same scenes as ourselves, wholly ignorant of the future and very imperfectly informed about the past, cannot tell at what moment the end ought to come. That it will come when it ought, we may be sure; but we waste our time in guessing when that will be. That it has a meaning we may be sure, but we cannot see it. When it is over, we may be told. We are led to expect that the Author will have something to say to each of us on the part that each of us has played. The playing it well is what matters infinitely.

What Are We to Make of Jesus Christ?

WHAT ARE WE TO MAKE of Jesus Christ? This is a question which has, in a sense, a frantically comic side. For the real question is not what are we to make of Christ, but what is He to make of us? The picture of a fly sitting deciding what it is going to make of an elephant has comic elements about it. But perhaps the questioner meant what are we to make of Him in the sense of "How are we to solve the historical problem set us by the recorded sayings and acts of this Man?" This problem is to reconcile two things. On the one hand you have got the almost generally admitted depth and sanity of His moral teaching, which is not very seriously questioned, even by those who are opposed to Christianity. In fact, I find when I am arguing with very anti-God people that they rather make a point of saying, "I am entirely in favor of the moral teaching of Christianity"—and there seems to be a general agreement that in the teaching of this Man and of His immediate followers, moral truth is exhibited at its purest and best. It is not sloppy idealism, it is full of wisdom and shrewdness. The whole thing is realistic, fresh to the highest degree, the product of a sane mind. That is one phenomenon.

The other phenomenon is the quite appalling nature of this Man's theological remarks. You all know what I mean, and I want to stress the point that the appalling claim which this Man seems to be making is not merely made at one moment of His career. There is, of course, the one moment which led to His execution. The moment at which the High

Priest said to Him, "Who are you?" "I am the Anointed, the Son of the uncreated God, and you shall see Me appearing at the end of all history as the judge of the Universe."

But that claim, in fact, does not rest on this one dramatic moment. When you look into his conversation, you will find this sort of claim running through the whole thing. For instance, He went about saying to people, "I forgive your sins." Now it is quite natural for a man to forgive something you do to *him*. Thus if somebody cheats *me* out of £5, it is quite possible and reasonable for me to say, "Well, I forgive him, we will say no more about it." What on earth would you say if somebody had done *you* out of £5 and *I* said, "That is all right, I forgive him"?

Then there is a curious thing which seems to slip out almost by accident. On one occasion this Man is sitting looking down on Jerusalem from the hill above it and suddenly in comes an extraordinary remark—"I keep on sending you prophets and wise men." Nobody comments on it. And yet, quite suddenly, almost incidentally, He is claiming to be the power that all through the centuries is sending wise men and leaders into the world.

Here is another curious remark: in almost every religion there are unpleasant observances like fasting. This Man suddenly remarks one day, "No one need fast while I am here." Who is this Man who remarks that His mere presence suspends all normal rules? Who is the person who can suddenly tell the School they can have a half-holiday?

Sometimes the statements put forward the assumption that He, the Speaker, is completely without sin or fault. This is always the attitude. "You, to whom I am talking, are all sinners," and He never remotely suggests that this same reproach can be brought against Him. He says again, "I am begotten of the One God, before Abraham was, I am," and remember what the words "I am" were in Hebrew. They were the name of God, which must not be spoken by any human being, the name which it was death to utter.

Well, that is the other side. On the one side clear, definite moral teaching. On the other, claims which, if not true, are those of a megalomaniac, compared with whom Hitler was the most sane and humble of men. There is no halfway house and there is no parallel in other religions. If you had gone to Buddha and asked him, "Are you the son of Bramah?" he would have said, "My son, you are still in the vale of illusion." If you had gone to Socrates and asked, "Are you Zeus?" he would have laughed at you. If you had gone to Mohammed and asked, "Are you Allah?" he would first have rent his clothes and then cut your head off. If you had asked Confucius, "Are you Heaven?" I think he would probably have replied, "Remarks which are not in accordance with nature are in bad taste." The idea of a great moral teacher saying what Christ said is out of the question. In my opinion, the only person who can say that sort of thing is either God or a complete lunatic suffering from that form of delusion which undermines the whole mind of man. If you think you are a poached egg when you are looking for a piece of toast to suit you, you may be sane, but if you think you are God, there is no chance for you.

We may note in passing that He was never regarded as a mere moral teacher. He did not produce that effect on any of the people who actually met Him. He produced mainly three effects—Hatred—Terror—Adoration. There was no trace of people expressing mild approval.

"Putting on Christ"

UP TILL NOW, I have been trying to describe facts—what God is and what He has done. Now I want to talk about practice—what do we do next? What difference does all this theology make? It can start making a difference tonight. If you are interested enough to have read thus far, you are probably interested enough to make a shot at saying your prayers; and, whatever else you say, you will probably say the Lord's Prayer.

Its very first words are *Our Father*. Do you now see what those words mean? They mean, quite frankly, that you are putting yourself in the place of a son of God. To put it bluntly, you are *dressing up as Christ*. If you like, you are pretending. Because, of course, the moment you realize what the words mean, you realize that you are not a son of God. You are not being like The Son of God, whose will and interests are at one with those of the Father: you are a bundle of self-centered fears, hopes, greeds, jealousies, and self-conceit, all doomed to death. So that, in a way, this dressing up as Christ is a piece of outrageous cheek. But the odd thing is that He has ordered us to do it.

Why? What is the good of pretending to be what you are not? Well, even on the human level, you know, there are two kinds of pretending. There is a bad kind, where the pretense is there instead of the real thing; as when a man pretends he is going to help you instead of really helping you. But there is also a good kind, where the pretense leads up to the real thing. When you are not feeling particularly friendly but know you ought to be, the best thing you can do, very often, is to put on a friendly manner and behave as if you were a nicer person than you actually are. And in a few minutes, as we have all noticed, you will be really feeling friendlier than you were. Very often the only way to get a quality in reality is to start behaving as if you had it already. That is why children's games are so important. They are always pretending to be grown-ups—playing soldiers, playing shop. But all the time, they are hardening their muscles and sharpening their wits, so that the pretense of being grown-up helps them to grow up in earnest.

Now the moment you realize "Here I am, dressing up as

Christ," it is extremely likely that you will see at once some way in which at that very moment the pretense could be made less of a pretense and more of a reality. You will find several things going on in your mind which would not be going on there if you were really a son of God. Well, stop them. Or you may realize that, instead of saying your prayers, you ought to be downstairs writing a letter, or helping your wife to wash up. Well, go and do it.

You see what is happening. The Christ Himself, the Son of God who is man (just like you) and God (just like His Father) is actually at your side and is already at that moment beginning to turn your pretense into a reality. This is not merely a fancy way of saying that your conscience is telling you what to do. If you simply ask your conscience, you get one result: if you remember that you are dressing up as Christ, you get a different one. There are lots of things which your conscience might not call definitely wrong (specially things in your mind) but which you will see at once you cannot go on doing if you are seriously trying to be like Christ. For you are no longer thinking simply about right and wrong; you are trying to catch the good infection from a Person. It is more like painting a portrait than like obeying a set of rules. And the odd thing is that while in one way it is much harder than keeping rules, in another way it is far easier.

The real Son of God is at your side. He is beginning to turn you into the same kind of thing as Himself. He is beginning, so to speak, to "inject" His kind of life and thought, His *Zoë*, into you; beginning to turn the tin soldier into a live man. The part of you that does not like it is the part that is still tin.

Perfection

WHEN I WAS A CHILD I often had [a] toothache, and I knew that if I went to my mother she would give me something which would deaden the pain for that night and let me get to sleep. But I did not go to my mother—at least, not till the pain became very bad. And the reason I did not go was this. I did not doubt she would give me the aspirin; but I knew she would also do something else. I knew she would take me to the dentist next morning. I could not get what I wanted out of her without getting something more, which I did not want. I wanted immediate relief from pain: but I could not get it without having my teeth set permanently right. And I knew those dentists; I knew they started fiddling about with all sorts of other teeth which had not yet begun to ache. They would not let sleeping dogs lie; if you gave them an inch, they took an ell.

Now, if I may put it that way, Our Lord is like the dentists. If you give Him an inch, He will take an ell. Dozens of people go to Him to be cured of some one particular sin which they are ashamed of (like masturbation or physical cowardice) or which is obviously spoiling daily life (like bad temper or drunkenness). Well, He will cure it all right: but He will not stop there. That may be all you asked; but if you once call Him in, He will give you the full treatment.

That is why He warned people to "count the cost" before becoming Christians. "Make no mistake," He says, "if you let Me, I will make you perfect. The moment you put yourself in My hands, that is what you are in for. Nothing less, or other, than that. You have free will, and if you choose, you can push Me away. But if you do not push Me away, understand that I am going to see this job through. Whatever suffering it may cost you in your earthly life, whatever inconceivable purification it may cost you after death, whatever it costs Me, I will never rest, nor let you rest, until you are literally perfect—until my Father can say without reservation that He is well pleased with you, as He said He was well pleased with Me. This I can do and will do. But I will not do anything less."

And yet—this is the other and equally important side of it—this Helper who will, in the long run, be satisfied with nothing less than absolute perfection, will also be delighted with the first feeble, stumbling effort you make tomorrow to do the simplest duty. As a great Christian writer (George Macdonald) pointed out, every father is pleased at the baby's first attempt to walk: no father would be satisfied with anything less than a firm, free, manly walk in a grown-up son. In the same way, he said, "God is easy to please, but hard to satisfy."

The practical upshot is this. On the one hand, God's demand for perfection need not discourage you in the least in your present attempts to be good, or even in your present failures. Each time you fall He will pick you up again. And He knows perfectly well that your own efforts are never going to bring you anywhere near perfection. On the other hand, you must realize from the outset that the goal toward which He is beginning to guide you is absolute perfection; and no power in the whole universe, except you yourself, can prevent Him from taking you to that goal. That is what you are in for. And it is very important to realize that.

First Fervor

MANY RELIGIOUS PEOPLE lament that the first fervors of their conversion have died away. They think—sometimes rightly, but not, I believe, always—that their sins account for this. They may even try by pitiful efforts of will to revive what now seem to have been the golden days. But were those fervors—the operative word is *those*—ever intended to last?

It would be rash to say that there is any prayer which God *never* grants. But the strongest candidate is the prayer we might express in the single word *encore*. And how should the Infinite repeat Himself? All space and time are too little for Him to utter Himself in them *once*.

And the joke, or tragedy, of it all is that these golden moments in the past, which are so tormenting if we erect them into a norm, are entirely nourishing, wholesome, and enchanting if we are content to accept them for what they are, for memories. Properly bedded down in a past which we do not miserably try to conjure back, they will send up exquisite growths. Leave the bulbs alone, and the new flowers will come up. Grub them up and hope, by fondling and sniffing, to get last year's blooms, and you will get nothing. "Unless a seed die. . . ."

Scruples

ONE MUSTN'T MAKE the Christian life into a punctilious system of *law*, like the Jewish, [for] two reasons. (1) It raises scruples when we don't keep the routine. (2) It raises presumption when we do. Nothing gives one a more spuriously good conscience than keeping rules, even if there has been a total absence of all real charity and faith.

Liturgy

EVERY SERVICE is a structure of acts and words through which we receive a sacrament, or repent, or supplicate, or adore. And it enables us to do these things best—if you like it, it "works" best—when, through long familiarity, we don't have to think about it. As long as you notice, and have to count, the steps, you are not yet dancing but only learning to dance. A good shoe is a shoe you don't notice. Good reading becomes possible when you need not consciously think about eyes, or light, or print, or spelling. The perfect church service would be the one we were almost unaware of; our attention would have been on God.

But every novelty prevents this. It fixes our attention on the service itself; and thinking about worship is a different thing from worshipping. The important question about the Grail was "for what does it serve?" " 'Tis mad idolatry that makes the service greater than the god."

A still worse thing may happen. Novelty may fix our attention not even on the service but on the celebrant. You know what I mean. Try as one may to exclude it, the question "What on earth is he up to now?" will intrude. It lays one's devotion waste. There is really some excuse for the man who said, "I wish they'd remember that the charge to Peter was Feed my sheep; not Try experiments on my rats, or even Teach my performing dogs new tricks."

Thus my whole liturgiological position really boils down to an entreaty for permanence and uniformity. I can make do with almost any kind of service whatever, if only it will stay put. But if each form is snatched away just when I am beginning to feel at home in it, then I can never make any progress in the art of worship. You give me no chance to acquire the trained habit—*habito dell'arte.*

It may well be that some variations which seem to me merely matters of taste really involve grave doctrinal differences. But surely not all? For if grave doctrinal differences are really as numerous as variations in practice, then we shall have to conclude that no such thing as the Church of England exists. And anyway, the Liturgical Fidget is not a purely Anglican phenomenon; I have heard Roman Catholics complain of it too. . . .

As to the words of the service—liturgy in the narrower sense—the question is rather different. If you have a vernacular liturgy, you must have a changing liturgy: otherwise it will finally be vernacular only in name. The ideal of "timeless English" is sheer nonsense. No living language can be timeless. You might as well ask for a motionless river.

I think it would have been best, if it were possible, that necessary change should have occurred gradually and (to most people) imperceptibly; here a little and there a little; one obsolete word replaced in a century—like the gradual change of spelling in successive editions of Shakespeare.

Holy Communion

IT IS ALMOST impossible to state the negative effect which certain doctrines have on me—my failure to be nourished by them—without seeming to mount an attack against them. But the very last thing I want to do is to unsettle in the mind of any Christian, whatever his denomination, the concepts—for him traditional—by which he finds it profitable to represent to himself what is happening when he receives the bread and wine. I could wish that no definitions had ever been felt to be necessary; and, still more, that none had been allowed to make divisions between churches.

Some people seem able to discuss different theories of this act as if they understood them all and needed only evidence as to which was best. This light has been withheld from me. I do not know and can't imagine what the disciples understood Our Lord to mean when, His body still unbroken and His blood unshed, He handed them the bread and wine, saying *they* were His body and blood. . . .

I hope I do not offend God by making my Communions in the frame of mind I have been describing. The command, after all, was Take, eat: not Take, understand. Particularly, I hope I need not be tormented by the question "What is this?"—this wafer, this sip of wine. That has a dreadful effect on me. It invites me to take "this" out of its holy context and regard it as an object among objects, indeed as part of nature. It is like taking a red coal out of the fire to examine it: it becomes a dead coal. To me, I mean. All this is autobiography, not theology.

Devotions to Saints

THERE IS CLEARLY a theological defense for it; if you can ask for the prayers of the living, why should you not ask for the prayers of the dead? There is clearly also a great danger. In some popular practice we see it leading off into an infinitely silly picture of Heaven as an earthly court where applicants will be wise to pull the right wires, discover the best "channels," and attach themselves to the most influential pressure groups. But I have nothing to do with all this. I am not thinking of adopting the practice myself; and who am I to judge the practice of others? . . .

The consoling thing is that while Christendom is divided about the rationality, and even the lawfulness, of praying *to* the saints, we are all agreed about praying *with* them. "With angels and archangels and all the company of heaven." . . . One always accepted this *with* theoretically. But it is quite different when one brings it into consciousness at an appropriate moment and wills the association of one's own little twitter with the voices of the great saints and (we hope) of our own dear dead. They may drown some of its uglier qualities and set off any tiny value it has.

You may say that the distinction between the communion of the saints as I find it in that act and full-fledged prayer to saints is not, after all, very great.

Church Music

THERE ARE TWO musical situations on which I think we can be confident that a blessing rests. One is where a priest or an organist, himself a man of trained and delicate taste, humbly and charitably sacrifices his own (esthetically right) desires and gives the people humbler and coarser fare than he would wish, in a belief (even, as it may be, the erroneous belief) that he can thus bring them to God. The other is where the stupid and unmusical layman humbly and patiently, and above all silently, listens to music which he cannot, or cannot fully, appreciate, in the belief that it somehow glorifies God, and that if it does not edify him this must be his own defect. Neither such a High Brow nor such a Low Brow can be far out of the way. To both, Church Music will have been a means of grace; not the music they have liked, but the music they have disliked. They have both offered, sacrificed, their taste in the fullest sense.

But where the opposite situation arises, where the musician is filled with pride of skill or the virus of emulation and looks with contempt on the unappreciative congregation, or where the unmusical, complacently entrenched in their own ignorance and conservatism, look with the restless and resentful hostility of an inferiority complex on all who would try to improve their taste—there, we may be sure, all that both offer is unblessed and the spirit that moves them is not the Holy Ghost.

Ready-made Prayers

FOR MANY YEARS after my conversion I never used any ready-made forms except the Lord's Prayer. In fact, I tried to pray without words at all—not to verbalize the mental acts. Even in praying for others I believe I tended to avoid their names and substituted mental images of them. I still think the prayer without words is the best—if one can really achieve it. But I now see that in trying to make it my daily bread I was counting on a greater mental and spiritual strength than I really have. To pray successfully without words one needs to be "at the top of one's form." Otherwise the mental acts become merely imaginative or emotional acts—and a fabricated emotion is a miserable affair. When the golden moments come, when God enables one really to pray without words, who but a fool would reject the gift? But He does not give it—anyway not to me—day in, day out. My mistake was what Pascal, if I remember rightly, calls "Error of Stoicism"; thinking we can do always what we can do sometimes. . . .

For me words are . . . secondary. They are only an anchor. Or, shall I say, they are the movements of a conductor's baton: not the music. They serve to canalize the worship, or penitence, or petition, which might without them—such are our minds—spread into wide and shallow puddles. It does not matter very much who first put them together. If they are our own words they will soon, by unavoidable repetition, harden into a formula. If they are someone else's, we shall continually pour into them our own meaning.

At present—for one's practice changes and, I think, ought

to change—I find it best to make "my own words" the staple but introduce a modicum of the ready-made. . . .

Perhaps I shan't find it so easy to persuade you that the ready-made modicum has . . . its use: for me, I mean—I'm not suggesting rules for anyone else in the world.

First, it keeps me in touch with "sound doctrine." Left to one's self, one could easily slide away from "the faith once given" into a phantom called "my religion."

Secondly, it reminds me "what things I ought to ask" (perhaps especially when I am praying for other people). The crisis of the present moment, like the nearest telegraph post, will always loom largest. Isn't there a danger that our great, permanent, objective necessities—often more important—may get crowded out?

Finally, they provide an element of the ceremonial.

Festooning Ready-made Prayers

I DON'T VERY MUCH like the job of telling you "more about my festoonings"—the private overtones I give to certain petitions. . . .

I call them "festoons," by the way, because they don't (I trust) obliterate the plain, public sense of the petition but are merely hung on it. . . .

Thy kingdom come. That is, may your reign be realized here, as it is realized there. But I tend to take *there* on three levels. First, as in the sinless world beyond the horrors of animal and human life; in the behavior of stars and trees and water, in sunrise and wind. May there be *here* (in my heart) the beginning of a like beauty. Secondly, as in the best human lives I have known: in all the people who really bear the burdens and ring true, and in the quiet, busy, ordered life of really good families and really good religious houses. May that too be "here." Finally, of course, in the usual sense: as in Heaven, as among the blessed dead.

And *here* can of course be taken not only as "in my heart," but as "in this college"—in England—in the world in general. But prayer is not the time for pressing our own favorite social or political panacea. Even Queen Victoria didn't like "being talked to as if she were a public meeting."

Thy will be done. My festoons on this have been added gradually. At first I took it exclusively as an act of submission, attempting to do with it what Our Lord did in Gethsemane. I thought of God's will purely as something that would come upon me, something of which I should be the patient. And I also thought of it as a will which would be embodied in pains and disappointments. Not, to be sure, that I supposed God's will for me to consist entirely of disagreeables. But I thought it was only the disagreeables that called for this preliminary submission—the agreeables could look after themselves for the present. When they turned up, one could give thanks.

This interpretation is, I expect, the commonest. And so it must be. And such are the miseries of human life that it must often fill our whole mind. But at other times other meanings can be added. So I added one more.

The peg for it is, I admit, much more obvious in the English version than in the Greek or Latin. No matter: this is where the liberty of festooning comes in. "Thy will *be done.*" But a great deal of it is to be done by God's creatures; including me. The petition, then, is not merely that I may patiently suffer God's will but also that I may vigorously do it. I must be an agent as well as a patient. I am asking that I may be enabled to do it. In the long run I am asking to be given "the same mind which was also in Christ."

Taken this way, I find the words have a more regular

daily application. For there isn't always—or we don't always have reason to suspect that there is—some great affliction looming in the near future, but there are always duties to be done; usually, for me, neglected duties to be caught up with. "Thy will be *done*—by me—now" brings one back to brass tacks.

But more than that, I am at this very moment contemplating a new festoon. Tell me if you think it a vain subtlety. I am beginning to feel that we need a preliminary act of submission not only toward possible future afflictions but also toward possible future blessings. I know it sounds fantastic; but think it over. It seems to me that we often, almost sulkily, reject the good that God offers us because, at that moment, we expected some other good. Do you know what I mean? On every level of our life—in our religious experience, in our gastronomic, erotic, esthetic, and social experience—we are always harking back to some occasion which seemed to us to reach perfection, setting that up as a norm, and depreciating all other occasions by comparison. But these other occasions, I now suspect, are often full of their own new blessing, if only we would lay ourselves open to it. God shows us a new facet of the glory, and we refuse to look at it because we're still looking for the old one. And of course we don't get that. You can't, at the twentieth reading, get again the experience of reading *Lycidas* for the first time. But what you do get can be in its own way as good.

When and Where to Pray

No ONE in his senses, if he has any power of ordering his own day, would reserve his chief prayers for bedtime—obviously the worst possible hour for any action which needs concentration. The trouble is that thousands of unfortunate people can hardly find any other. . . . My own plan, when hard pressed, is to seize any time, and place, however unsuitable, in preference to the last waking moment. On a day of traveling—with, perhaps, some ghastly meeting at the end of it—I'd rather pray sitting in a crowded train than put it off till midnight when one reaches a hotel bedroom with aching head and dry throat and one's mind partly in a stupor and partly in a whirl. On other, and slightly less crowded, days a bench in a park, or a back street where one can pace up and down, will do.

A man to whom I was explaining this said, "But why don't you turn into a church?" Partly because, for nine months of the year, it will be freezingly cold, but also because I have had bad luck with churches. No sooner do I enter one and compose my mind than one or other of two things happens. Either someone starts practicing the organ. Or else, with resolute tread, there appears from nowhere a pious woman in elastic side-boots, carrying mop, bucket, and dustpan, and begins beating hassocks and rolling up carpets and doing things to flower vases. Of course (blessings on her) "work is prayer," and her enacted *oratio* is probably worth ten times my spoken one. But it doesn't help mine to become worth more.

When one prays in strange places and at strange times, one can't kneel, to be sure. I won't say this doesn't matter. The body ought to pray as well as the soul. Body and soul are both the better for it. Bless the body. Mine has led me into many scrapes, but I've led it into far more. If the imagination were obedient, the appetite would give us very little trouble. And from how much it has saved me! And but for our body one whole realm of God's glory—all that we receive through the senses—would go unpraised. For the beasts can't appreciate it and the angels are, I suppose, pure intelligences. They *understand* colors and tastes better than our greatest scientists; but have they retinas or palates? I

fancy the "beauties of nature" are a secret God has shared
with us alone. That may be one of the reasons why we were
made—and why the resurrection of the body is an important doctrine.

But I'm being led into a digression. . . . The relevant
point is that kneeling does matter, but other things matter
even more. A concentrated mind and a sitting body make
for better prayer than a kneeling body and a mind half
asleep. Sometimes these are the only alternatives. . . .

A clergyman once said to me that a railway compartment,
if one has it to one's self, is an extremely good place to pray
in "because there is just the right amount of distraction."
When I asked him to explain, he said that perfect silence
and solitude left one more open to the distractions which
come from within, and that a moderate amount of external
distraction was easier to cope with. I don't find this so myself, but I can imagine it.

The Moment of Prayer

WE ARE ALWAYS, completely, and therefore equally, known
to God. That is our destiny whether we like it or not. But
though this knowledge never varies, the quality of our
being known can. A school of thought holds that "freedom
is willed necessity." Never mind if they are right or not. I
want this idea only as an analogy. Ordinarily, to be known
by God is to be, for this purpose, in the category of things.
We are like earthworms, cabbages, and nebulae, objects of
divine knowledge. But when we (a) become aware of the
fact—the present fact, not the generalization—and (b) assent with all our will to be so known, then we treat ourselves, in relation to God, not as things but as persons. We

have unveiled. Not that any veil could have baffled this sight. The change is in us. The passive changes to the active. Instead of merely being known, we show, we tell, we offer ourselves to view.

To put ourselves thus on a personal footing with God could, in itself and without warrant, be nothing but presumption and illusion. But we are taught that it is not; that it is God who gives us that footing. For it is by the Holy Spirit that we cry "Father." By unveiling, by confessing our sins and "making known" our requests, we assume the high rank of persons before Him. And He, descending, becomes a Person to us.

But I should not have said "becomes." In Him there is no becoming. He reveals Himself as Person: or reveals that in Him which is Person. For—dare one say it? in a book it would need pages of qualification and insurance—God is in some measure to a man as that man is to God. The door in God that opens is the door he knocks at. (At least, I think so usually.) The Person in Him—He is more than a person— meets those who can welcome or at least face it. He speaks as "I" when we truly call Him "Thou." (How good Buber is!)

This talk of "meeting" is, no doubt, anthropomorphic; as if God and I could be face to face, like two fellow creatures, when in reality He is above me and within me and below me and all about me. That is why it must be balanced by all manner of metaphysical and theological abstractions. But never, here or anywhere else, let us think that while anthropomorphic images are a concession to our weakness, the abstractions are the literal truth. Both are equally concessions; each singly misleading, and the two together mutually corrective. Unless you sit to it very tightly, continually murmuring "Not thus, not thus, neither is this Thou," the abstraction is fatal. It will make the life of lives inanimate and the love of loves impersonal. The naive image is mischievous chiefly insofar as it holds unbelievers back from conversion. It does believers, even at its crudest, no harm. What soul ever perished for believing that God the Father really has a beard?

Mechanics of Meditation

WHAT IS MORE NATURAL, and easier, if you believe in God, than to address Him: How could one not?

Yes. But it depends who one is. For those in my position—adult converts from the *intelligentsia*—that simplicity and spontaneity can't always be the starting point. One can't just jump back into one's childhood. If one tries to, the result will only be an archaizing revival, like Victorian Gothic—a parody of being born again. We have to work back to the simplicity a long way round.

In actual practice, in my prayers, I often have to use that long way at the very beginning of the prayer.

St. François de Sales begins every meditation with the command *Mettez-vous en la présence de Dieu.* I wonder how many different mental operations have been carried out in intended obedience to that?

What happens to me if I try to take it . . . simply, is the juxtaposition of two "representations," or ideas, or phantoms. One is the bright blur in the mind which stands for God. The other is the idea I call "me." But I can't leave it at that, because I know—and it's useless to pretend I don't know—that they are both phantasmal. The real I has created them both—or, rather, built them up in the vaguest way from all sorts of psychological odds and ends.

St. Ignatius Loyola (I think it was) advised his pupils to begin their meditations with what he called a *compositio loci.* The Nativity or the Marriage at Cana, or whatever the theme might be, was to be visualized in the fullest possible detail. One of his English followers would even have us look up "what good Authors write of those places" so as to get the topography, "the height of the hills and the situation of the townes," correct. Now for two different reasons this is not "addressed to my condition."

One is that I live in an archaeological age. We can no longer, as St. Ignatius could, believingly introduce the clothes, furniture, and utensils of our own age into ancient Palestine. I'd know I wasn't getting them right. I'd know that the very sky and sunlight of those latitudes were different from any my northern imagination could supply. I could no doubt pretend to myself a naiveté I don't really possess; but that would cast an unreality over the whole exercise.

The second reason is more important. St. Ignatius was a great master, and I am sure he knew what his pupils needed. I conclude that they were people whose visual imagination was weak and needed to be stimulated. But the trouble with people like ourselves is the exact reverse. We can say this to one another because, in our mouths, it is not a boast but a confession. We are agreed that the power—indeed, the compulsion—to visualize is not "Imagination" in the higher sense, not the Imagination which makes a man either a great author or a sensitive reader. Ridden on a very tight rein, this visualizing power can sometimes serve true Imagination; very often it merely gets in the way.

If I started with a *compositio loci*, I should never reach the meditation. The picture would go on elaborating itself indefinitely and becoming every moment of less spiritual relevance. . . .

I have called my material surroundings a stage set. A stage set is not a dream nor a nonentity. But if you attack a stage house with a chisel, you will not get chips of brick or stone; you'll only get a hole in a piece of canvas and, beyond that, windy darkness. Similarly, if you start investigating the nature of matter, you will not find anything like what imagination has always supposed matter to be. You will get mathematics. From that unimaginable physical reality my senses select a few stimuli. These they translate or symbolize into sensations, which have no likeness at all to the reality of matter. Of these sensations my associative power, very much directed by my practical needs and influenced by social training, makes up little bundles into what I call "things" (labeled by nouns). Out of these I build myself a neat little box stage, suitably provided with properties such as hills, fields, houses, and the rest. In this I can act.

And you may well say "act." For what I call "myself" (for all practical, everyday purposes) is also a dramatic construction; memories, glimpses in the shaving glass, and snatches of the very fallible activity called "introspection" are the principal ingredients. Normally I call this construction "me," and the stage set "the real world."

Now the moment of prayer is for me—or involves for me as its condition—the awareness, the reawakened awareness, that this "real world" and "real self" are very far from being rock-bottom realities. I cannot, in the flesh, leave the stage, either to go behind the scenes or to take my seat in the pit; but I can remember that these regions exist. And I also remember that my apparent self—the clown, or hero, or super—under his greasepaint is a real person with an off-stage life. The dramatic person could not tread the stage unless he concealed a real person: unless the real and unknown I existed, I would not even make mistakes about the imagined me. And in prayer this real I struggles to speak, for once, from his real being, and to address, for once, not the other actors, but—what shall I call Him: The Author, for He invented us all? The Producer, for He controls all? Or the Audience, for He watches, and will judge, the performance?

The attempt is not to escape from space and time and from my creaturely situation as a subject facing objects. It is more modest: to reawake the awareness of that situation. If that can be done, there is no need to go anywhere else. This situation itself is, at every moment, a possible theophany. Here is the holy ground; the Bush is burning now.

Answered Prayers

THE NEW TESTAMENT contains embarrassing promises that what we pray for with faith we shall receive. Mark 11:24 is the most staggering. Whatever we ask for, believing that we'll get it, we'll get. No question, it seems, of confining it to spiritual gifts; *whatever* we ask for. No question of a merely general faith in God, but a belief that you will get the particular thing you ask. No question of getting either it or else something that is really far better for you; you'll get precisely it. . . .

How is this astonishing promise to be reconciled (a) with the observed facts? and (b) with the prayer in Gethsemane, and (as a result of that prayer) the universally accepted view that we should ask everything with a reservation ("if it be Thy will")?

As regards (a), no evasion is possible. Every war, every famine or plague, almost every deathbed, is the monument to a petition that was not granted. . . .

But (b), though much less often mentioned, is surely an equal difficulty. How is it possible at one and the same moment to have a perfect faith—an untroubled or unhesitating faith as St. James says (1:6)—that you will get what you ask and yet also prepare yourself submissively in advance for possible refusal? If you envisage a refusal as possible, how can you have simultaneously a perfect confidence that what you ask will not be refused? If you have that confidence, how can you take refusal into account at all?

It is easy to see why so much more is written about worship and contemplation than about "crudely" or "naively" petitionary prayer. They may be—I think they are—nobler forms of prayer. But they are also a good deal easier to write about. . . .

It seems to me we must conclude that such promises about prayer with faith refer to a degree or kind of faith which most believers never experience. A far inferior degree is, I hope, acceptable to God. Even the kind that says "Help Thou my unbelief" may make way for a miracle. Again, the absence of such faith as insures the granting of the prayer is not even necessarily a sin; for Our Lord had no such assurance when He prayed in Gethsemane.

The Efficacy of Prayer

SOME YEARS AGO I got up one morning intending to have my hair cut in preparation for a visit to London, and the first letter I opened made it clear I need not go to London. So I decided to put the haircut off too. But then there began the most unaccountable little nagging in my mind, almost like a voice saying, "Get it cut all the same. Go and get it cut." In the end I could stand it no longer. I went. Now my barber at that time was a fellow Christian and a man of many troubles whom my brother and I had sometimes been able to help. The moment I opened his shop door he said, "Oh, I was praying you might come today." And, in fact, if I had come a day or so later, I should have been of no use to him.

It awed me; it awes me still. But, of course, one cannot

rigorously prove a causal connection between the barber's prayers and my visit. It might be telepathy. It might be accident.

I have stood by the bedside of a woman whose thighbone was eaten through with cancer and who had thriving colonies of the disease in many other bones as well. It took three people to move her in bed. The doctors predicted a few months of life; the nurses (who often know better), a few weeks. A good man laid his hands on her and prayed. A year later the patient was walking (uphill, too, through rough woodland) and the man who took the last X-ray photos was saying, "These bones are as solid as rock. It's miraculous."

But once again there is no rigorous proof. Medicine, as all true doctors admit, is not an exact science. We need not invoke the supernatural to explain the falsification of its prophecies. You need not, unless you choose, believe in a causal connection between the prayers and the recovery.

The question then arises, "What sort of evidence *would* prove the efficacy of prayer?" The thing we pray for may happen, but how can you ever know it was not going to happen anyway? Even if the thing were indisputably miraculous, it would not follow that the miracle had occurred because of your prayers. The answer surely is that a compulsive empirical proof such as we have in the sciences can never be attained.

Some things are proved by the unbroken uniformity of our experiences. The law of gravitation is established by the fact that, in our experience, all bodies without exception obey it. Now even if all the things that people prayed for happened, which they do not, this would not prove what Christians mean by the efficacy of prayer. For prayer is request. The essence of request, as distinct from compulsion, is that it may or may not be granted. And if an infinitely wise Being listens to the requests of finite and foolish creatures, of course He will sometimes grant and sometimes refuse them. Invariable "success" in prayer would not prove the Christian doctrine at all. It would prove something much more like magic—a power in certain human beings to control, or compel, the course of nature.

There are, no doubt, passages in the New Testament which may seem at first sight to promise an invariable granting of our prayers. But that cannot be what they really mean. For in the very heart of the story we meet a glaring instance to the contrary. In Gethsemane the holiest of all petitioners prayed three times that a certain cup might pass from Him. It did not. After that the idea that prayer is recommended to us as a sort of infallible gimmick may be dismissed.

Other things are proved not simply by experience but by those artificially contrived experiences which we call experiments. Could this be done about prayer? I will pass over the objection that no Christian could take part in such a project, because he has been forbidden it: "You must not try experiments on God, your Master." Forbidden or not, is the thing even possible?

I have seen it suggested that a team of people—the more the better—should agree to pray as hard as they knew how, over a period of six weeks, for all the patients in Hospital A and none of those in Hospital B. Then you would tot up the results and see if A had more cures and fewer deaths. And I suppose you would repeat the experiment at various times and places so as to eliminate the influence of irrelevant factors.

The trouble is that I do not see how any real prayer could go on under such conditions. "Words without thoughts never to heaven go," says the King in *Hamlet*. Simply to say prayers is not to pray; otherwise a team of properly trained parrots would serve as well as men for our experiment. You cannot pray for the recovery of the sick unless the end you have in view is their recovery. But you can have no motive for desiring the recovery of all the patients in one hospital and none of those in another. You are not doing it in order that suffering should be relieved; you are doing it to find out what happens. The real purpose and the nominal purpose of your prayers are at variance. In other words, whatever your tongue and teeth and knees may do, you are not praying. The experiment demands an impossibility.

Empirical proof and disproof are, then, unobtainable. But this conclusion will seem less depressing if we remember that prayer is request and compare it with other specimens of the same thing.

We make requests of our fellow creatures as well as of God: we ask for the salt, we ask for a raise in pay, we ask a friend to feed the cat while we are on our holidays, we ask a woman to marry us. Sometimes we get what we ask for and sometimes not. But when we do, it is not nearly so easy as one might suppose to prove with scientific certainty a causal connection between the asking and the getting.

Your neighbor may be a humane person who would not have let your cat starve even if you had forgotten to make any arrangement. Your employer is never so likely to grant your request for a raise as when he is aware that you could get better money from a rival firm and is quite possibly intending to secure you by a raise in any case. As for the lady who consents to marry you—are you sure she had not decided to do so already? Your proposal, you know, might have been the result, not the cause, of her decision. A certain important conversation might never have taken place unless she had intended that it should.

Thus in some measure the same doubt that hangs about the causal efficacy of our prayers to God hangs also about our prayers to man. Whatever we get we might have been going to get anyway. But only, as I say, in some measure. Our friend, boss, and wife may tell us that they acted because we asked and we may know them so well as to feel sure, first that they are saying what they believe to be true, and secondly that they understand their own motives well enough to be right. But notice that when this happens our assurance has not been gained by the methods of science. We do not try the control experiment of refusing the raise or breaking off the engagement and then making our request again under fresh conditions. Our assurance is quite different in kind from scientific knowledge. It is born out of our personal relation to the other parties; not from knowing things about them but from knowing *them*.

Our assurance—if we reach an assurance—that God always hears and sometimes grants our prayers, and that apparent grantings are not merely fortuitous, can only come in the same sort of way. There can be no question of tabulating successes and failures and trying to decide whether the successes are too numerous to be accounted for by chance. Those who best know a man best know whether, when he did what they asked, he did it because they asked. I think those who best know God will best know whether He sent me to the barber's shop because the barber prayed.

Mysticism

THE FOLLOWING POSITION is gaining ground and is extremely plausible. Mystics (it is said) starting from the most diverse religious premises all find the same things. These things have singularly little to do with the professed doctrines of any particular religion—Christianity, Hinduism, Buddhism, Neo-Platonism, etc. Therefore, mysticism is, by empirical evidence, the only real contact man has ever had with the unseen. The agreement of the explorers proves that they are all in touch with something objective. It is therefore the one true religion. And what we call the "religions" are either mere delusions or, at best, so many porches through which an entrance into transcendent reality can be effected.

> And when he hath the kernel eate,
> Who doth not throw away the shell?

I am doubtful about the premises. Did Plotinus and Lady Julian and St. John of the Cross really find "the same things"? Even admitting some similarity. One thing common to all mysticisms is the temporary shattering of our ordinary spatial and temporary consciousness and of our discursive intellect. The value of this negative experience must depend on the nature of that positive, whatever it is, for which it makes room. But should we not expect that the negative would always *feel* the same? If wineglasses were conscious, I suppose that *being emptied* would be the same experience for each, even if some were to remain empty, and some to be filled with poison, and some broken. All who leave the land and put to sea will find "the same things"—the land sinking below the horizon, the gulls dropping behind, the salty breeze. Tourists, merchants, sailors, pirates, missionaries—it's all one. But this identical experience vouches for nothing about the utility or lawfulness or final event of their voyages.

> It may be that the gulfs will wash them down,
> It may be they will touch the Happy Isles.

I do not at all regard mystical experience as an illusion. I think it shows that there is a way to go, before death, out of what may be called "this world"—out of the stage set. Out of this; but into what? That's like asking an Englishman "Where does the sea lead to?" He will reply, "To everywhere on earth, including Davy Jones's locker, except England." The lawfulness, safety, and utility of the mystical voyage depends not at all on its being mystical—that is, on its being a departure—but on the motives, skill, and constancy of the voyager, and on the grace of God. The true religion gives value to its own mysticism; mysticism does not validate the religion in which it happens to occur.

I shouldn't be at all disturbed if it could be shown that a diabolical mysticism, or drugs, produced experiences indistinguishable (by introspection) from those of the great Christian mystics. Departures are all alike; it is the landfall that crowns the voyage. The saint, by being a saint, proves that his mysticism (if he was a mystic; not all saints are) led him aright; the fact that he has practiced mysticism could never prove his sanctity.

Spiritual Reading

WHEREVER YOU FIND a little study circle of Christian laity, you can be almost certain that they are studying not St. Luke, or St. Paul, or St. Augustine, or Thomas Aquinas, or Hooker, or Butler, but M. Berdyaev, or M. Maritain, or Mr. Niebuhr, or Miss Sayers, or even myself.

Now this seems to me topsy-turvy. Naturally, since I myself am a writer, I do not wish the ordinary reader to read no modern books. But I would advise him to read the old. And I would give him this advice precisely because he is an amateur and therefore much less protected against the dangers of an exclusive contemporary diet. A new book is still on its trial and the amateur is not in a position to judge it. It has to be tested against the great body of Christian thought down the ages, and all its hidden implications (often unsuspected by the author himself) have to be brought to light. Often it cannot be fully understood without the knowledge of a good many other modern books. If you join at eleven o'clock a conversation which began at eight, you will often not see the real bearing of what is said.

Remarks which seem to you very ordinary will produce laughter or irritation and you will not see why—the reason, of course, being that the earlier stages of the conversation have given them a special point. In the same way sentences in a modern book which look quite ordinary may be directed "at" some other book; in this way you may be led to accept what you would have indignantly rejected if you knew its real significance. The only safety is to have a standard of plain, central Christianity ("mere Christianity" as Baxter called it) which puts the controversies of the moment in their proper perspective. Such a standard can be acquired only from the old books. It is a good rule, after reading a new book, never to allow yourself another new one till you have read an old one in between. If that is too much for you, you should at least read one old one to every three new ones.

✳

For a good ("popular") defense of our position against modern woffle, to fall back on, I know nothing better than G. K. Chesterton's *The Everlasting Man*. Harder reading, but very protective, is Edwyn Bevan's *Symbolism and Belief*. Charles Williams's *He Came Down from Heaven* doesn't suit everyone, but try it.

For meditative and devotional reading (a little bit at a time, more like sucking a lozenge than eating a slice of bread), I suggest *The Imitation of Christ* (astringent) and Traherne's *Centuries of Meditation* (joyous). Also my selection from Macdonald, *George Macdonald: An Anthology*. I can't read Kierkegaard myself, but some people find him helpful.

For Christian morals I suggest my wife's (Joy Davidman) *Smoke on the Mountain;* Gore's *The Sermon on the Mount* and (perhaps) his *Philosophy of the Good Life*. And possibly (but with a grain of salt, for he is too puritanical) William Law's *Serious Call to a Devout and Holy Life. . . .*

You'll want mouthwash for the *imagination*. I'm told that Mauriac's novels (all excellently translated, if your French is rusty) are good, though very severe. Dorothy Sayers' *Man Born to be King* (those broadcast plays) certainly is. So, to me, but not to everyone, are Charles Williams's fantastic novels. *Pilgrim's Progress,* if you ignore some straw-splitting dialogues on Calvinist theology and concentrate on the story, is first-class.

St. Augustine's *Confessions* will give you the record of an earlier adult convert, with many very great devotional passages intermixed.

Do you read poetry? George Herbert at his best is extremely nutritious.

I don't mention the Bible because I take that for granted. A modern translation is for most purposes far more useful than the Authorized Version.

As regards my own books, you might (or might not) care for *Transposition, The Great Divorce,* or *The Four Loves.* . . .

Have you read anything by an American Trappist called Thomas Merton? I'm at present on his *No Man Is an Island.* It is the best new spiritual reading I've met for a long time.

✳

About prides, superiorities, and affronts, there's no book better than Law's *Serious Call to a Devout and Holy Life* where you'll find all of us pinned like butterflies on cards—the cards being little stories of typical characters in the most sober, astringent eighteenth-century prose.

Reading the Gospels

EVERYONE TOLD ME that [in the Gospels] I should find a figure whom I couldn't help loving. Well, I could. They told me I would find moral perfection—but one sees so very little of Him in ordinary situations that I couldn't make much of that either. Indeed some of His behavior seemed to me open to criticism, e.g. accepting an invitation to dine with a Pharisee and then loading him with torrents of abuse. Now the truth is, I think, that the sweetly-attractive-human-Jesus is a product of nineteenth-century skepticism, produced by people who were ceasing to believe in His divinity but wanted to keep as much Christianity as they could. It is not what an unbeliever coming to the records with an open mind will (at first) find there. The first thing you find is that we are simply not *invited* to speak, to pass any moral judgment on Him, however favorable; it is only too clear that He is going to do whatever judging there is; it is *we* who are *being* judged, sometimes tenderly, sometimes with stunning severity, but always *de haut en bas*. (Have you ever noticed that your imagination can hardly be forced to picture Him as shorter than yourself?) The first real work of the Gospels on a fresh reader is, and ought to be, to raise very acutely the question, "Who or What is this?" For there is a good deal in the character which, unless He really is what He says he is, is not lovable or even tolerable. If He *is*, then of course it is another matter; nor will it then be surprising if much remains puzzling to the end. For if there is anything in Christianity, we are now approaching something which will never be fully comprehensible. On this whole aspect of the subject I should go on . . . to Chesterton's *Everlasting Man*. You might also find Mauriac's *Vie de Jesus* useful. . . . If childish associations are too intrusive, in reading the New Testament it's a good idea to try it in some other language, or Moffatt's translation.

Biblical Exegesis

SCRIPTURE DOESN'T TAKE the slightest pain to guard the doctrine of Divine Impassibility. We are constantly represented as exciting the Divine wrath or pity—even as "grieving" God. I know this language is analogical. But when we say that, we must not smuggle in the idea that we can throw the analogy away and, as it were, get in behind it to a purely literal truth. All we can really substitute for the analogical expression is some theological abstraction. And the abstraction's value is almost entirely negative. It warns us against drawing absurd consequences from the analogical expression by prosaic extrapolations. By itself, the abstraction "impassible" can get us nowhere. It might even suggest something far more misleading than the most naive Old Testament picture of a stormily emotional Jehovah. Either something inert, or something which was "Pure Act" in such a sense that it could take no account of events within the universe it had created.

I suggest two rules for exegetics. (1) Never take the images literally. (2) When the *purport* of the images—what they say to our fear, and hope, and will, and affections— seems to conflict with the theological abstractions, trust the purport of the images every time. For our abstract thinking is itself a tissue of analogies: a continual modeling of spiritual reality in legal, or chemical, or mechanical terms. Are these likely to be more adequate than the sensuous, organic, and personal images of Scripture—light and darkness, river and well, seed and harvest, master and servant, hen and chickens, father and child? The footprints of the Divine are more visible in that rich soil than across rocks or slag heaps. Hence what they now call "demythologizing"

Christianity can easily be "remythologizing" it—and substituting a poorer mythology for a richer.

Thought, Imagination, Language

WHEN I THINK about London, I usually see a mental picture of Euston Station. But when I think (as I do) that London has several million inhabitants, I do not mean that there are several million images of people contained in my image of Euston Station. Nor do I mean that several millions of real people live in the real Euston Station. In fact, though I have the image while I am thinking about London, what I think or say is not *about* that image, and would be manifest nonsense if it were. It makes sense because it is not about my own mental pictures but about the real London, outside my imagination, of which no one can have an adequate mental picture at all. Or again, when we say that the Sun is ninety-odd million miles away, we understand perfectly clearly what we mean by this number; we can divide and multiply it by other numbers and we can work out how long it would take to travel that distance at any given speed. But this clear *thinking* is accompanied by *imagining* which is ludicrously false to what we know that the reality must be.

To think, then, is one thing, and to imagine is another. What we think or say can be, and usually is, quite different from what we imagine or picture; and what we mean may be true when the mental images that accompany it are entirely false. It is, indeed, doubtful whether anyone except an extreme visualist who is also a trained artist ever has mental images which are particularly like the things he is thinking about.

In these examples the mental image is not only unlike the reality but is known to be unlike it, at least after a moment's reflection. I know that London is not merely Euston Station. Let us now go on to a slightly different predicament. I once heard a lady tell her young daughter that you would die if you ate too many tablets of aspirin. "But why?" asked the child, "it isn't poisonous." "How do you know it isn't poisonous?" said the mother. "Because," said the child, "when you crush an aspirin tablet you don't find horrid red things inside it." Clearly, when this child thought of poison, she had a mental picture of Horrid Red Things, just as I have a picture of Euston when I think of London. The difference is that whereas I know my image to be very unlike the real London, the child thought that poison was *really* red. To that extent she was mistaken. But this does not mean that everything she thought or said about poison was necessarily nonsensical. She knew perfectly well that a poison was something which killed you or made you ill if you swallowed it; and she knew, to some extent, which of the substances in her mother's house were poisonous. If a visitor to that house had been warned by the child, "Don't drink that. Mother says it is poison," he would have been ill-advised to neglect the warning on the ground that "This child has a primitive idea of poison as Horrid Red Things, which my adult scientific knowledge has long since refuted."

We can now add to our previous statement (that thinking may be sound where the images that accompany it are false) the further statement: thinking may be sound in certain respects where it is accompanied not only by false images but by false images mistaken for true ones.

There is still a third situation to be dealt with. In our two previous examples we have been concerned with thought and imagination, but not with language. I had to picture Euston Station, but I did not need to *mention* it; the child thought that poison was Horrid Red Things, but she could talk about poison without saying so. But very often, when we are talking about something which is not perceptible by the five senses, we use words which, in one of their meanings, refer to things or actions that are. When a man says that he grasps an argument, he is using a verb (*grasp*) which literally means to take something in the hands, but he is certainly not thinking that his mind has hands or that an argument can be seized like a gun. To avoid the word *grasp* he may change the form of expression and say, "I see your point," but he does not mean that a pointed object has appeared in his visual field. He may have a third shot and say, "I follow you," but he does not mean that he is walking behind you along a road. Everyone is familiar with this linguistic phenomenon and the grammarians call it metaphor. But it is a serious mistake to think that metaphor is an optional thing which poets and orators may put into their work as a decoration and plain speakers can do without. The truth is that if we are going to talk at all about things which are not perceived by the senses, we are forced to use language metaphorically. Books on psychology, or economics, or politics are as continuously metaphorical as books of poetry or devotion. There is no other way of talking, as every philologist is aware. Those who wish can satisfy themselves on the point by reading the books I have already mentioned [Mr. Owen Barfield's *Poetic Diction* and Mr. Edwyn Bevan's *Symbolism and Belief*] and the other books to which those two will lead them on. It is a study for a lifetime and I must here content myself with the mere statement; all speech about supersensibles is, and must be, metaphorical in the highest degree.

We have now three guiding principles before us. (1) That thought is distinct from the imagination which accompanies it. (2) That thought may be in the main sound even when false images that accompany it are mistaken by the thinker for true ones. (3) That anyone who talks about things that cannot be seen, or touched, or heard, or the like, must inevitably talk as *if they could be* seen, or touched, or heard (for example, must talk of "complexes" and "repressions" *as if* institutions could really grow like trees or unfold like flowers; of energy being "released" *as if* it were an animal let out of a cage).

Scripture

IF EVEN PAGAN UTTERANCES can carry a second meaning, not quite accidentally but because . . . they have a sort of right to it, we shall expect the Scriptures to do this more momentously and more often. We have two grounds for doing so if we are Christians.

(1) For us these writings are "holy," or "inspired," or, as St. Paul says, "the Oracles of God." But this has been understood in more than one way, and I must try to explain how I understand it, at least so far as the Old Testament is concerned. I have been suspected of being what is called a Fundamentalist. That is because I never regard any narrative as unhistorical simply on the ground that it includes the miraculous. Some people find the miraculous so hard to believe that they cannot imagine any reason for my acceptance of it other than a prior belief that every sentence of the Old Testament has historical and scientific truth. But this I do not hold, any more than St. Jerome did when he said that Moses described Creation "after the manner of a popular poet" (as we should say, mythically) or than Calvin did when he doubted whether the story of Job were history or fiction. The real reason why I can accept as historical a story in which a miracle occurs is that I have never found any philosophical grounds for the universal negative proposition that miracles do not happen. I have to decide on other grounds (if I decide at all) whether a given narrative is

historical or not. The Book of Job appears to me unhistorical because it begins about a man quite unconnected with all history or even legend, with no genealogy, living in a country of which the Bible elsewhere has hardly anything to say; because, in fact, the author quite obviously writes as a storyteller not as a chronicler.

I have therefore no difficulty in accepting, say, the view of those scholars who tell us that the account of Creation in Genesis is derived from earlier Semitic stories which were Pagan and mythical. We must, of course, be quite clear what "derived from" means. Stories do not reproduce their species like mice. They are told by men. Each reteller either repeats exactly what his predecessor had told him or else changes it. He may change it unknowingly or deliberately. If he changes it deliberately, his invention, his sense of form, his ethics, his ideas of what is fit, or edifying, or merely interesting, all come in. If unknowingly, then his unconscious (which is so largely responsible for our forgettings) has been at work. Thus at every step in what is called—a little misleadingly—the "evolution" of a story, a man, all he is and all his attitudes, are involved. And no good work is done anywhere without aid from the Father of Lights. When a series of such retellings turns a creation story which at first had almost no religious or metaphysical significance into a story which achieves the idea of true Creation and of a transcendent Creator (as Genesis does), then nothing will make me believe that some of the re-tellers, or some one of them, has not been guided by God. . . .

(2) The second reason for accepting the Old Testament in this way can be put more simply and is, of course, far more compulsive. We are committed to it in principle by Our Lord Himself. On that famous journey to Emmaus He found fault with the two disciples for not believing what the prophets had said. They ought to have known from their Bibles that the Anointed One, when He came, would enter

His glory through suffering. He then explained, from "Moses" (that is, the Pentateuch) down, all the places in the Old Testament "concerning Himself" (Luke 24:25–27). He clearly identified Himself with a figure often mentioned in the Scriptures; appropriated to Himself many passages where a modern scholar might see no such reference. In the predictions of His Own Passion which He had previously made to the disciples, He was obviously doing the same thing. He accepted—indeed He claimed to be—the second meaning of Scripture.

We do not know—or anyway I do not know—what all these passages were. We can be pretty sure about one of them. The Ethiopian eunuch who met Philip (Acts 8:27–38) was reading Isaiah 53. He did not know whether in that passage the prophet was talking about himself or about someone else. Philip, in answering his question, "preached unto him Jesus." The answer, in fact, was "Isaiah is speaking of Jesus." We need have no doubt that Philip's authority for this interpretation was Our Lord. . . . We can, again, be pretty sure, from the words on the cross (Mark 15:34), that Our Lord identified Himself with the sufferer in Psalm 22. Or when He asked (Mark 12:35,36) how Christ could be both David's son and David's Lord, He clearly identified Christ, and therefore Himself, with the "my Lord" of Psalm 110—was in fact hinting at the mystery of the Incarnation by pointing out a difficulty which only it could solve. In Matthew 4:6 the words of Psalm 91:11,12, "He shall give his angels charge over thee . . . that thou hurt not thy foot against a stone," are applied to Him, and we may be sure the application was His own since only He could be the source of the temptation story. In Mark 12:10 He implicitly appropriates to Himself the words of Psalm 118:22 about the stone which the builders rejected. "Thou shalt not leave my soul in hell, neither shalt thou suffer thy Holy One to see corruption" (Psalm 16:11) is treated as a prophecy of His resurrection in Acts 2:27, and was doubtless so taken by Himself, since we find it so taken in the earliest Christian tradition—that is, by people likely to be closer both to the spirit and to the letter of His words than any scholarship (I do not say, "any sanctity") will bring a modern. Yet it is, perhaps, idle to speak here of spirit and letter. There is almost no "letter" in the words of Jesus. Taken by a literalist, He will always prove the most elusive of teachers. Systems cannot keep up with that darting illumination. No net less wide than a man's whole heart, nor less fine of mesh than love, will hold the sacred Fish.

The Psalms

THE PSALMS ARE POEMS, and poems intended to be sung: not doctrinal treatises, nor even sermons. Those who talk of reading the Bible "as literature" sometimes mean, I think, reading it without attending to the main thing it is about; like reading Burke with no interest in politics, or reading the *Aeneid* with no interest in Rome. That seems to me to be nonsense. But there is a saner sense in which the Bible, since it is, after all, literature, cannot properly be read except as literature; and the different parts of it as the different sorts of literature they are. Most emphatically the Psalms must be read as poems; as lyrics, with all the licenses and all the formalities, the hyperboles, the emotional rather than logical connections, which are proper to lyric poetry. They must be read as poems if they are to be understood; no less than French must be read as French or English as English. Otherwise we shall miss what is in them and think we see what is not.

Their chief formal characteristic, the most obvious element of pattern, is fortunately one that survives in translation. Most readers will know that I mean what the scholars call "parallelism"; that is, the practice of saying the same thing twice in different words. A perfect example is "He that dwelleth in heaven shall laugh them to scorn: the Lord shall have them in derision" (2:4), or again, "He shall make thy righteousness as clear as the light; and thy just dealing as the noonday" (37:6). If this is not recognized as pattern, the reader will either find mares' nests (as some of the older preachers did) in his effort to get a different meaning out of each half of the verse or else feel that it is rather silly.

In reality it is a very pure example of what all pattern, and therefore all art, involves. The principle of art has been defined by someone as "the same in the other." Thus in a country dance you take three steps and then three steps again. That is the same. But the first three are to the right and the second three to the left. That is the other. In a building there may be a wing on one side and a wing on the other, but both of the same shape. . . . "Parallelism" is the characteristically Hebrew form of the same in the other, but it occurs in many English poets too: for example, in Marlowe's

> Cut is the branch that might have grown full straight
> And burned is Apollo's laurel bough,

or in the childishly simple form used by the *Cherry Tree Carol,*

> Joseph was an old man and an old man was he.

Of course, the Parallelism is often partially concealed on purpose (as the balances between masses in a picture may be something far subtler than complete symmetry). And, of course, other and more complex patterns may be worked in across it, as in Psalm 119, or in 107 with its refrain. I mention only what is most obvious, the Parallelism itself. It is (according to one's point of view) either a wonderful piece of luck or a wise provision of God's, that poetry which was to be turned into all languages should have as its chief formal characteristic one that does not disappear (as mere meter does) in translation.

If we have any taste for poetry, we shall enjoy this feature of the Psalms. Even those Christians who cannot enjoy it will respect it; for Our Lord, soaked in the poetic tradition of His country, delighted to use it. "For with what judgment ye judge, ye shall be judged; and with what measure ye mete, it shall be measured to you again" (Matthew 7:2). The second half of the verse makes no logical addition; it echoes, with variation, the first, "Ask, and it shall be given to you; seek, and ye shall find; knock, and it shall be opened unto you" (Matthew 7:7). The advice is given in the first phrase, then twice repeated with different images. We may, if we like, see in this an exclusively practical and didactic purpose; by giving to truths which are infinitely worth remembering this rhythmic and incantatory expression, He made them almost impossible to forget. I like to suspect more. It seems to me appropriate, almost inevitable, that when that great Imagination which in the beginning, for Its own delight and for the delight of men and angels and (in their proper mode) of beasts, had invented and formed the whole world of Nature, submitted to express Itself in human speech, that speech should sometimes be poetry. For poetry too is a little incarnation, giving body to what had been before invisible and inaudible.

Prayer of Praise

WHEN I FIRST BEGAN to draw near to belief in God and even for some time after it had been given to me, I found a stumbling block in the demand so clamorously made by all religious people that we should "praise" God; still more in the suggestion that God Himself demanded it. We all despise the man who demands continued assurance of his own virtue, intelligence, or delightfulness; we despise still more the crowd of people round every dictator, every millionaire, every celebrity, who gratify that demand. Thus a picture, at once ludicrous and horrible, both of God and of His worshipers, threatened to appear in my mind. The Psalms were especially troublesome in this way—"Praise the Lord," "O praise the Lord with me," "Praise Him." (And why, incidentally, did praising God so often consist in telling other people to praise Him? Even in telling whales, snowstorms, etc., to go on doing what they would certainly do whether we told them or not?) Worse still was the statement put into God's own mouth, "whoso offereth me thanks and praise, he honoreth me" (Psalm 50:23). It was hideously like saying, "What I most want is to be told that I am good and great." Worst of all was the suggestion of the very silliest Pagan bargaining, that of the savage who makes offerings to his idol when the fishing is good and beats it when he has caught nothing. More than once the Psalmist seemed to be saying, "You like praise. Do this for me, and you shall have some." Thus in Psalm 54 the poet begins "save me" (verse 1), and in verse 6 adds an inducement, "An offering of a free heart will I give thee, and praise thy Name." Again and again the speaker asks to be saved from death on the ground that if God lets His suppliants die, He will get no more praise from them, for the ghost in Sheol cannot praise (Psalm 30:10; Psalm 88:10; Psalm 119:175). And mere quantity of praise seemed to count; "seven times a day do I praise thee" (Psalm 119:164). It was extremely distressing. It made one think what one least wanted to think. Gratitude to God, reverence to Him, obedience to Him, I thought I could understand; not this perpetual eulogy. Nor were matters mended by a modern author who talked of God's "right" to be praised.

I still think "right" is a bad way of expressing it, but I believe I now see what that author meant. It is perhaps easiest to begin with inanimate objects which can have no rights. What do we mean when we say that a picture is "admirable"? We certainly don't mean that it is admired (that's as may be) for bad work is admired by thousands and good work may be ignored. Nor that it "deserves" admiration in the sense in which a candidate "deserves" a high mark from the examiners—that is, that a human being will have suffered injustice if it is not awarded. The sense in which the picture "deserves" or "demands" admiration is rather this; that admiration is the correct, adequate or appropriate, response to it, that, if paid, admiration will not be "thrown away," and that if we do not admire we shall be stupid, insensible, and great losers, we shall have missed something. In that way many objects both in Nature and in Art may be said to deserve, or merit, or demand, admiration. It was from this end, which will seem to some irreverent, that I found it best to approach the idea that God "demands" praise. He is that Object to admire which (or, if you like, to appreciate which) is simply to be awake, to have entered the real world; not to appreciate which is to have lost the greatest experience, and in the end to have lost all. The incomplete and crippled lives of those who are tone deaf, have never been in love, never known true friendship, never cared for a good book, never enjoyed the feel of the morning air on their cheeks, never (I am one of these) enjoyed football, are faint images of it.

But, of course, this is not all. God does not only "demand" praise as the supremely beautiful and all-satisfying Object. He does apparently command it as lawgiver. The Jews were told to sacrifice. We are under an obligation to go to church. But this was a difficulty only because I did not . . . see that it is in the process of being worshiped that God communicates His presence to men. It is not, of course, the only way. But for many people at many times the "fair beauty of the Lord" is revealed briefly or only while they worship Him together. Even in Judaism the essence of the sacrifice was not really that men gave bulls and goats to God, but that by their so doing God gave Himself to men; in the central act of our own worship, of course, this is far clearer—there it is manifestly, even physically, God who gives and we who receive. The miserable idea that God should in any sense need, or crave for, our worship like a vain woman wanting compliments, or a vain author presenting his new books to people who never met or heard of him, is implicitly answered by the words "If I be hungry I will not tell *thee*" (Psalm 50:12). Even if such an absurd Deity could be conceived, He would hardly come to *us*, the lowest of rational creatures, to gratify His appetite. I don't want my dog to bark approval of my books. Now that I come to think of it, there are some humans whose enthusiastically favorable criticism would not much gratify me.

But the most obvious fact about praise—whether of God or anything—strangely escaped me. I thought of it in terms of compliment, approval, or the giving of honor. I had never noticed that all enjoyment spontaneously overflows into praise unless (sometimes even if) shyness or the fear of boring others is deliberately brought in to check it. The world rings with praise—lovers praising their mistresses, readers praising their favorite poet, walkers praising the countryside, players praising their favorite game—praise of weather, wines, dishes, actors, motors, horses, colleges, countries, historical personages, children, flowers, mountains, rare stamps, rare beetles, even sometimes politicians or scholars. I had not noticed how the humblest, and at the same time most balanced and capacious minds, praised most, while the cranks, misfits, and malcontents praised least. The good critics found something to praise in many imperfect works; the bad ones continually narrowed the list of books we might be allowed to read. The healthy and unaffected man, even if luxuriously brought up and widely experienced in good cookery, could praise a very modest meal: the dyspeptic and the snob found fault with all. Except where intolerably adverse circumstances interfere, praise almost seems to be inner health made audible. Nor does it cease to be so when, through lack of skill, the forms of its expression are very uncouth or even ridiculous. Heaven knows, many poems of praise addressed to an earthly beloved are as bad as our bad hymns, and an anthology of love poems for public and perpetual use would probably be as sore a trial to literary taste as *Hymns Ancient and Modern*. I had not noticed, either, that just as men spontaneously praise whatever they value, so they spontaneously urge us to join them in praising it: "Isn't she lovely? Wasn't it glorious? Don't you think that magnificent?" The Psalmists in telling everyone to praise God are doing what all men do when they speak of what they care about. My whole, more general, difficulty about the praise of God depended on my absurdly denying to us, as regards the supremely Valuable, what we delight to do, what indeed we can't help doing, about everything else we value.

I think we delight to praise what we enjoy because the praise not merely expresses but completes the enjoyment; it is its appointed consummation. It is not out of compliment that lovers keep on telling one another how beautiful they are; the delight is incomplete till it is expressed. It is frustrating to have discovered a new author and not to be able to tell anyone how good he is; to come suddenly, at the turn of the road, upon some mountain valley of unexpected grandeur and then to have to keep silent because the people with you care for it no more than for a tin can in the ditch; to hear a good joke and find no one to share it with (the perfect hearer died a year ago). This is so even when our expressions are inadequate, as, of course, they usually are. But how if one could really and fully praise even such things to perfection—utterly "get out" in poetry, or music, or paint the upsurge of appreciation which almost bursts you? Then indeed the object would be fully appreciated and our delight would have attained perfect development. The worthier the object, the more intense this delight would be. If it were possible for a created soul fully (I mean, up to the full measure conceivable in a finite being) to "appreciate," that is to love and delight in, the worthiest object of all, and simultaneously at every moment to give this delight perfect expression, then that soul would be in supreme beatitude. It is along these lines that I find it easiest to understand the Christian doctrine that "Heaven" is a state in which angels now, and men hereafter, are perpetually employed in praising God. This does not mean, as it can so dismally suggest, that it is like "being in Church." For our "services," both in their conduct and in our power to participate, are merely attempts at worship; never fully successful, often 99.9 percent failures; sometimes total failures. We are not riders but pupils in the riding school; for most of us the falls and bruises, the aching muscles, and the severity of the exercise, far outweigh those few moments in which we were, to our own astonishment, actually galloping without terror and without disaster. To see what the doctrine really means, we must suppose ourselves to be in perfect love with God—drunk with, drowned in, dissolved by, that delight which, far from remaining pent up within ourselves as incommunicable, hence hardly tolerable, bliss, flows out from us incessantly again in effortless and perfect expression, our joy no more separable from the praise in which it liberates and utters itself than the brightness a mirror receives is separable from the brightness it sheds. The Scotch catechism says that man's chief end is "to glorify God and enjoy Him forever." But we shall then know that these are the same thing. Fully to enjoy is to glorify. In commanding us to glorify Him, God is inviting us to enjoy Him.

Modern Translations of the Bible

IT IS POSSIBLE that the reader . . . may ask himself why we need a new translation of any part of the Bible. . . . "Do we not already possess," it may be said, "in the Authorized Version the most beautiful rendering which any language can boast?" Some people whom I have met go even further and feel that a modern translation is not only unnecessary but even offensive. They cannot bear to see the time-honored words altered; it seems to them irreverent.

There are several answers to such people. In the first place, the kind of objection which they feel to a new translation is very like the objection which was once felt to any English translation at all. Dozens of sincerely pious people in the sixteenth century shuddered at the idea of turning the time-honored Latin of the Vulgate into our common and (as they thought) "barbarous" English. A sacred truth seemed to them to have lost its sanctity when it was stripped of the polysyllabic Latin, long heard at Mass and at Hours, and put into "language such as men do use"—language steeped in all the commonplace associations of the nursery, the inn, the stable, and the street. The answer then was the same as the answer now. The only kind of sanctity which Scripture can lose (or, at least, New Testament Scripture) by being modernized is an accidental kind which it never had for its writers or its earliest readers. The New Testament in the original Greek is not a work of literary art: it is not written in a solemn, ecclesiastical language; it is written in the sort of Greek which was spoken over the

Eastern Mediterranean after Greek had become an international language and therefore lost its real beauty and subtlety. In it we see Greek used by people who have no real feeling for Greek words because Greek words are not the words they spoke when they were children. It is a sort of "basic" Greek; a language without roots in the soil, a utilitarian, commercial, and administrative language. Does this shock us? It ought not to, except as the Incarnation itself ought to shock us. The same divine humility which decreed that God should become a baby at a peasant woman's breast, and later an arrested field preacher in the hands of the Roman police, decreed also that He should be preached in a vulgar, prosaic, and unliterary language. If you can stomach the one, you can stomach the other. The Incarnation is in that sense an irreverent doctrine. When we expect that it should have come before the World in all the beauty that we now feel in the Authorized Version, we are as wide of the mark as the Jews were in expecting that the Messiah would come as a great earthly King. The real sanctity, the real beauty and sublimity of the New Testament (as of Christ's life) are of a different sort: miles deeper and *further in*.

In the second place, the Authorized Version has ceased to be a good (that is, a clear) translation. It is no longer modern English: the meanings of words have changed. The same antique glamor which has made it (in the superficial sense) so "beautiful," so "sacred," so "comforting," and so "inspiring," has also made it in many places unintelligible. Thus where St. Paul says, "I know nothing against myself," it translates "I know nothing by myself" (1 Corinthians 4:4). That was a good translation (though even then rather old-fashioned) in the sixteenth century: to the modern reader it means either nothing, or something quite different from what St. Paul said. The truth is that if we are to have translation at all, we must have periodical retranslation. There is no such thing as translating a book into another language once and for all, for a language is a changing thing. If your son is to have clothes, it is no good buying him a suit once and for all: he will grow out of it and have to be reclothed.

And finally—though it may seem a sour paradox—we must sometimes get away from the Authorized Version if for no other reason, simply *because* it is so beautiful and so solemn. Beauty exalts, but beauty also lulls. Early associations endear but they also confuse. Through that beautiful solemnity the transporting or horrifying realities of which the Book tells may come to us blunted and disarmed and we may only sigh with tranquil veneration when we ought to be burning with shame, or struck dumb with terror, or carried out of ourselves by ravishing hopes and adorations.

Moral Choices

PEOPLE OFTEN THINK of Christian morality as a kind of bargain in which God says, "If you keep a lot of rules, I'll reward you, and if you don't I'll do the other thing." I do not think that is the best way of looking at it. I would much rather say that every time you make a choice you are turning the central part of you, the part of you that chooses, into something a little different from what it was before. And taking your life as a whole, with all your innumerable choices, all your life long you are slowly turning this central thing either into a Heaven creature or into a hellish creature: either into a creature that is in harmony with God, and with other creatures, and with itself, or else into one that is in a state of war and hatred with God, and with its fellow creatures, and with itself. To be the one kind of creature is Heaven: that is, it is joy, and peace, and knowledge, and power. To be the other means madness, horror, idiocy, rage, impotence, and eternal loneliness. Each of us at each moment is progressing to the one state or the other.

Virtue

THERE IS A DIFFERENCE between doing some particular just or temperate action and being a just or temperate man. Someone who is not a good tennis player may now and then make a good shot. What you mean by a good player is the man whose eye and muscles and nerves have been so trained by making innumerable good shots that they can now be relied on. They have a certain tone or quality which is there even when he is not playing, just as a mathematician's mind has a certain habit and outlook which is there even when he is not doing mathematics. In the same way a man who perseveres in doing just actions gets in the end a certain quality of character. Now it is that quality rather than the particular actions which we mean when we talk of "virtue."

Prudence

PRUDENCE MEANS practical common sense, taking the trouble to think out what you are doing and what is likely to come of it. Nowadays most people hardly think of Prudence as one of the "virtues." In fact, because Christ said we could only get into His world by being like children, many Christians have the idea that, provided you are "good," it does not matter being a fool. But that is a misunderstanding. In the first place, most children show plenty of "prudence" about doing the things they are really interested in, and think them out quite sensibly. In the second place, as St. Paul points out, Christ never meant that we were to remain children in *intelligence*: on the contrary, He told us to be not only "as harmless as doves" but also "as wise as serpents." He wants a child's heart, but a grown-up's head. He wants us to be simple, single-minded, affectionate, and teachable, as good children are; but He also wants every bit of intelligence we have to be alert at its job, and in first-class fighting trim. The fact that you are giving money to a charity does not mean that you need not try to find out whether that charity is a fraud or not. The fact that what you are thinking about is God Himself (for example, when you are praying) does not mean that you can be content with the same babyish ideas which you had when you were a five-year-old. It is, of course, quite true that God will not love you any the less, or have less use for you, if you happen to have been born with a very second-rate brain. He has room for people with very little sense, but He wants everyone to use what sense they have. The proper motto is not "Be good, sweet maid, and let who can be clever," but "Be good, sweet maid, and don't forget that this involves being as clever as you can." God is no fonder of intellectual slackers than of any other slackers.

Temperance

TEMPERANCE IS, unfortunately, one of those words that has changed its meaning. It now usually means teetotalism. But in the days when the second Cardinal virtue was christened

"Temperance," it meant nothing of the sort. Temperance referred not specially to drink, but to all pleasures; and it meant not abstaining, but going the right length and no further. It is a mistake to think that Christians ought all to be teetotalers; Mohammedanism, not Christianity, is the teetotal religion. Of course it may be the duty of a particular Christian, or of any Christian, at a particular time, to abstain from strong drink either because he is the sort of man who cannot drink at all without drinking too much, or because he wants to give the money to the poor, or because he is with people who are inclined to drunkenness and must not encourage them by drinking himself. But the whole point is that he is abstaining, for a good reason, from something which he does not condemn and which he likes to see other people enjoying. One of the marks of a certain type of bad man is that he cannot give up a thing himself without wanting everyone else to give it up. That is not the Christian way. An individual Christian may see fit to give up all sorts of things for special reasons—marriage, or meat, or beer, or the cinema; but the moment he starts saying the things are bad in themselves, or looking down his nose at other people who do use them, he has taken the wrong turning.

Justice and Fortitude

JUSTICE MEANS much more than the sort of thing that goes on in law courts. It is the old name for everything we should now call "fairness"; it includes honesty, give and take, truthfulness, keeping promises, and all that side of life. And Fortitude includes both kinds of courage—the kind that faces danger as well as the kind that "sticks it" under pain. "Guts" is perhaps the nearest modern English. You will notice, of course, that you cannot practice any of the other virtues very long without bringing this one into play.

Chastity

CHASTITY IS the most unpopular of the Christian virtues. There is no getting away from it: the old Christian rule is, "Either marriage, with complete faithfulness to your partner, or else total abstinence." Now this is so difficult and so contrary to our instincts, that obviously either Christianity is wrong or our sexual instinct, as it now is, has gone wrong. One or the other. Of course, being a Christian, I think it is the instinct which has gone wrong.

But I have other reasons for thinking so. The biological purpose of sex is children, just as the biological purpose of eating is to repair the body. Now if we eat whenever we feel inclined and just as much as we want, it is quite true that most of us will eat too much: but not terrifically too much. One man may eat enough for two, but he does not eat enough for ten. The appetite goes a little beyond its biological purpose, but not enormously. But if a healthy young man indulged his sexual appetite whenever he felt inclined, and if each act produced a baby, then in ten years he might easily populate a small village. This appetite is in ludicrous and preposterous excess of its function.

Or take it another way. You can get a large audience together for a striptease act—that is, to watch a girl undress on the stage. Now suppose you came to a country where you could fill a theater by simply bringing a covered plate on to the stage and then slowly lifting the cover so as to let everyone see, just before the lights went out, that it contained a mutton chop or a bit of bacon, would you not think that in that country something had gone wrong with the appetite for food? And would not anyone who had grown up in a different world think there was something equally queer about the state of the sex instinct among us? . . .

Here is a third point. You find very few people who want to eat things that really are not food or to do other things with food instead of eating it. In other words, perversions of the food appetite are rare. But perversions of the sex instinct are numerous, hard to cure, and frightful. I am sorry to have to go into [this], but I must. The reason why I must is that you and I, for the last twenty years, have been fed all day long on good solid lies about sex. We have been told, till one is sick of hearing it, that sexual desire is in the same state as any of our other natural desires and that if only we abandon the silly old Victorian idea of hushing it up, everything in the garden will be lovely. It is not true. The moment you look at the facts, and away from the propaganda, you see that it is not.

Belief

ROUGHLY SPEAKING, the word Faith seems to be used by Christians in two senses or on two levels, and I will take them in turn. In the first sense it means simply Belief—accepting or regarding as true the doctrines of Christianity. That is fairly simple. But what does puzzle people—at least it used to puzzle me—is the fact that Christians regard Faith in this sense as a virtue. I used to ask how on Earth it can be a virtue—what is there moral or immoral about believing or not believing a set of statements? Obviously, I used to say, a sane man accepts or rejects any statement, not because he wants or does not want to, but because the evidence seems to him good or bad. If he were mistaken about the goodness or badness of the evidence, that would not mean he was a bad man, but only that he was not very clever. And if he thought the evidence bad but tried to force himself to believe in spite of it, that would be merely stupid.

Well, I think I still take that view. But what I did not see then—and a good many people do not see still—was this. I was assuming that if the human mind once accepts a thing as true it will automatically go on regarding it as true, until some real reason for reconsidering it turns up. In fact, I was assuming that the human mind is completely ruled by reason. But that is not so. For example, my reason is perfectly convinced by good evidence that anesthetics do not smother me and that properly trained surgeons do not start operating until I am unconscious. But that does not alter the fact that when they have me down on the table and clap their horrible mask over my face, a mere childish panic begins inside me. I start thinking I am going to choke, and I am afraid they will start cutting me up before I am properly under. In other words, I lose my faith in anesthetics. It is not reason that is taking away my faith: on the contrary, my faith is based on reason. It is my imagination and emotions. The battle is between faith and reason on one side and emotion and imagination on the other. . . .

Now just the same thing happens about Christianity. I am not asking anyone to accept Christianity if his best reasoning tells him that the weight of evidence is against it. That is not the point at which Faith comes in. But supposing a man's reason once decides that the weight of the evidence is for it. I can tell that man what is going to happen to him in the next few weeks. There will come a moment when there is bad news, or he is in trouble, or is living among a lot of other people who do not believe it, and all at once his emotions will rise up and carry out a sort of blitz on his belief. Or else there will come a moment when he wants a woman, or wants to tell a lie, or feels very pleased with himself, or sees a chance of making a little money in some way that is not perfectly fair: some moment, in fact, at which it would be very convenient if Christianity were not true. And once again his wishes and desires will carry out a blitz. I am not talking of moments at which any real new reasons against Christianity turn up. Those have to be faced and that is a different matter. I am talking about moments where a mere mood rises up against it.

Now Faith, in the sense in which I am here using the word, is the art of holding onto things your reason has once accepted, in spite of your changing moods. For moods will change, whatever view your reason takes. I know that by experience. Now that I am a Christian, I do have moods in which the whole thing looks very improbable: but when I was an atheist, I had moods in which Christianity looked terribly probable. This rebellion of your moods against your real self is going to come anyway. That is why Faith is such a necessary virtue: unless you teach your moods "where they get off," you can never be either a sound Christian or even a sound atheist, but just a creature dithering to and fro, with its beliefs really dependent on the weather and the state of its digestion. Consequently one must train the habit of Faith.

Belief and Disbelief

IN ACTUAL MODERN English usage the verb "believe," except for two special usages, generally expresses a very weak degree of opinion. "Where is Tom?" "Gone to London, I believe." The speaker would be only mildly surprised if Tom had not gone to London after all. "What was the date?" "430 B.C., I believe." The speaker means that he is far from sure. It is the same with the negative if it is put in the form "I believe not." ("Is Jones coming up this term?" "I believe not.") But if the negative is put in a different form, it then becomes one of the special usages I mentioned a moment ago. This is of course the form "I don't believe it," or the still stronger "I don't believe you." "I don't believe it" is far stronger on the negative side than "I believe" is on the positive. "Where is Mrs. Jones?" "Eloped with the butler, I believe." "I don't believe it." This, especially if said with anger, may imply a conviction which in subjective certitude might be hard to distinguish from knowledge by experience. The other special usage is "I believe" as uttered by a Christian. There is no great difficulty in making the hardened materialist understand, however little he approves, the sort of mental attitude which this "I believe" expresses. The materialist need only picture himself replying, to some report of a miracle, "I don't believe it," and then imagine this same degree of conviction on the opposite side. He knows that he cannot, there and then, produce a refutation of the miracle which would have the certainty of mathematical demonstration; but the formal possibility that the miracle might after all have occurred does not really trouble him any more than a fear that water might not be H and O. Similarly, the Christian does not necessarily claim to have demonstrative proof; but the formal possibility that God might not exist is not necessarily present in the form of the least actual doubt. Of course there are Christians who hold that such demonstrative proof exists, just as there may be materialists who hold that there is demonstrative disproof. But then, whichever of them is right (if either is) while he retained the proof or disproof would be not believing or disbelieving but knowing. We are speaking of belief and disbelief in the strongest degree, but not of knowledge.

Belief, in this sense, seems to me to be assent to a proposition which we think so overwhelmingly probable that there is a psychological exclusion of doubt, though not a logical exclusion of dispute.

It may be asked whether belief (and of course disbelief) of this sort ever attaches to any but theological propositions. I think that many beliefs approximate to it; that is, many probabilities seem to us so strong that the absence of logical certainty does not induce in us the least shade of doubt. The scientific beliefs of those who are not themselves scientists often have this character, especially among the uneducated. Most of our beliefs about other people are of the same sort. The scientist himself, or he who was a scientist in the laboratory, has beliefs about his wife and friends which he holds, not indeed without evidence, but with more certitude than the evidence, if weighed in the laboratory manner, would justify. Most of my generation had a belief in the reality of the external world and of other people—if you prefer it, a disbelief in solipsism—far in excess of our strongest arguments. It may be true, as they now say, that the whole thing arose from category mistakes and was a pseudo-problem; but then we didn't know that in the twenties. Yet we managed to disbelieve in solipsism all the same.

There is, of course, no question so far of belief without evidence. We must beware of confusion between the way in which a Christian first assents to certain propositions and the way in which he afterward adheres to them. These must be carefully distinguished. Of the second it is true, in a sense, to say that Christians do recommend a certain discounting of apparent contrary evidence, and I will later attempt to explain why. But so far as I know it is not expected that a man should assent to these propositions in the first place without evidence or in the teeth of the evidence. At any rate, if anyone expects that, I certainly do not. And in fact, the man who accepts Christianity always thinks he had good evidence; whether, like Dante, *fisici e metafisici argomenti*, or historical evidence, or the evidence of religious experience, or authority, or all these together. For of course authority, however we may value it in this or that particular instance, is a kind of evidence. All of our historical beliefs, most of our geographical beliefs, many of our beliefs about matters that concern us in daily life, are accepted on the authority of other human beings, whether we are Christians, Atheists, Scientists, or Men-in-the-Street.

Faith

THE QUESTION of Faith . . . arises after a man has tried his level best to practice the Christian virtues, and found that he fails, and seen that even if he could he would only be giving back to God what was already God's own. In other words, he discovers his bankruptcy. Now, once again, what God cares about is not exactly our actions. What he cares about is that we should be creatures of a certain kind of quality—the kind of creatures He intended us to be—creatures related to Himself in a certain way. I do not add "and related to one another in a certain way" because that is included: if you are right with Him, you will inevitably be right with all your fellow creatures, just as if all the spokes of a wheel are fitted rightly into the hub and the rim, they are bound to be in the right positions to one another. And as long as a man is thinking of God as an Examiner who has set him a sort of paper to do, or as the opposite party in a sort of bargain—as long as he is thinking of claims and counterclaims between himself and God—he is not yet in the right relation to Him. He is misunderstanding what he is and what God is. And he cannot get into the right relation until he has discovered the fact of our bankruptcy.

When I say "discovered," I mean really discovered: not simply said it parrot-fashion. Of course, any child, if given a certain kind of religious education, will soon learn to *say* that we have nothing to offer to God that is not already His own and that we find ourselves failing to offer even that without keeping something back. But I am talking of really discovering this: really finding out by experience that it is true.

Now we cannot, in that sense, discover our failure to keep God's law except by trying our very hardest (and then failing). Unless we really try, whatever we say there will always be at the back of our minds the idea that, if we try harder next time, we shall succeed in being completely good. Thus, in one sense, the road back to God is a road of moral effort, of trying harder and harder. But in another sense it is not trying that is ever going to bring us home. All this trying leads up to the vital moment at which you turn to God and say, "You must do this. I can't." Do not, I implore you, start asking yourselves, "Have I reached that moment?" Do not sit down and start watching your own mind to see if it is coming along. That puts a man quite on the wrong track. When the most important things in our life happen, we quite often do not know, at the moment, what is going on. A man does not always say to himself, "Hullo! I'm growing up." You can see it even in simple matters. A man who starts anxiously watching to see whether he is going to sleep is very likely to remain wide awake. As well, the thing I am talking of now may not happen to everyone in a sudden flash—as it did to St. Paul or Bunyan: it may be so gradual that no one could ever point to a particular hour or even a particular year. And what matters is the nature of the change in itself, not how we feel while it is happening. It is the change from being confident about our own efforts to the state in which we despair of doing anything for ourselves and leave it to God.

Faith and Good Works

CHRISTIANS HAVE often disputed as to whether what leads the Christian home is good actions, or Faith in Christ. I have no right really to speak on such a difficult question, but it does seem to me like asking which blade in a pair of scissors is [more] necessary. A serious moral effort is the only thing that will bring you to the point where you throw up the sponge. Faith in Christ is the only thing to save you from despair at that point: and out of that Faith in Him good actions must inevitably come. There are two parodies of the truth which different sets of Christians have, in the past, been accused by other Christians of believing: perhaps they may make the truth clearer. One set [was] accused of saying, "Good actions are all that matters. The best good action is charity. The best kind of charity is giving money. The best thing to give money to is the Church. So hand us over £10,000 and we will see you through." The answer to that nonsense, of course, would be that good actions done for that motive, done with the idea that Heaven can be bought, would not be good actions at all, but only commercial speculations. The other set [was] accused of saying, "Faith is all that matters. Consequently, if you have faith, it doesn't matter what you do. Sin away, my lad, and have a good time and Christ will see that it makes no difference in the end." The answer to that nonsense is that, if what you call your "faith" in Christ does not involve taking the slightest notice of what He says, then it is not Faith at all—not faith or trust in Him, but only intellectual acceptance of some theory about Him.

The Bible seems to clinch the matter when it puts the two things together into one amazing sentence. The first half is, "Work out your own salvation with fear and trembling"— which looks as if everything depended on us and our good actions: but the second half goes on. "For it is God who worketh in you"—which looks as if God did everything and we nothing. I am afraid this is the sort of thing we come up against in Christianity. I am puzzled, but I am not surprised. You see, we are now trying to understand, and to separate into watertight compartments, what exactly God does and what man does when God and man are working together. And, of course, we begin by thinking it is like two men working together, so that you could say, "He did this bit and I did that." But this way of thinking breaks down. God is not like that. He is inside you as well as outside: even if we could understand who did what, I do not think human language could properly express it. In the attempt to express it, different Churches say different things. But you will find that even those who insist most strongly on the importance of good actions tell you you need Faith; and even those who insist most strongly on Faith tell you to do good actions. At any rate that is as far as I go.

Good Work and Good Works

"GOOD WORKS" in the plural is an expression much more familiar to modern Christendom than "good work." Good works are chiefly almsgiving or "helping" in the parish. They are quite separate from one's "work." And good works need not be good work, as anyone can see by inspecting some of the objects made to be sold at bazaars for charitable purposes. This is not according to our example.

When our Lord provided a poor wedding party with an extra glass of wine all around, he was doing good works. But also good work; it was a wine really worth drinking. Nor is the neglect of goodness in our "work," our job, according to precept. The apostle says everyone must not only work but work to produce what is "good."

The idea of Good Work is not quite extinct among us, though it is not, I fear, especially characteristic of religious people. I have found it among cabinetmakers, cobblers, and sailors. It is no use at all trying to impress sailors with a new liner because she is the biggest or costliest ship afloat. They look for what they call her "lines": they predict how she will behave in a heavy sea. Artists also talk of Good Work; but decreasingly. They begin to prefer words like "significant," "important," "contemporary," or "daring." These are not, to my mind, good symptoms.

But the great mass of men in all fully industrialized societies are the victims of a situation which almost excludes the idea of Good Work from the outset. "Built-in obsolescence" becomes an economic necessity. Unless an article is so made that it will go to pieces in a year or two and thus have to be replaced, you will not get a sufficient turnover. A hundred years ago, when a man got married, he had built for him (if he were rich enough) a carriage in which he expected to drive for the rest of his life. He now buys a car which he expects to sell again in two years. Work nowadays must *not* be good.

For the wearer, zip fasteners have this advantage over buttons: that, while they last, they will save him an infinitesimal amount of time and trouble. For the producer, they have a much more solid merit; they don't remain in working order long. Bad work is the *desideratum*.

We must avoid taking a glibly moral view of this situation. It is not solely the result of original or actual sin. It has stolen upon us, unforeseen and unintended. The degraded commercialism of our minds is quite as much its result as its cause. Nor can it, in my opinion, be cured by purely moral efforts.

Hope

HOPE IS ONE of the Theological virtues. This means that a continual looking forward to the eternal world is not (as some modern people think) a form of escapism or wishful thinking, but one of the things a Christian is meant to do. It does not mean that we are to leave the present world as it is. If you read history you will find that the Christians who did most for the present world were just those who thought most of the next. The Apostles themselves, who set on foot the conversion of the Roman Empire, the great men who built up the Middle Ages, the English Evangelicals who abolished the Slave Trade, all left their mark on Earth, precisely because their minds were occupied with Heaven. It is since Christians have largely ceased to think of the other world that they have become so ineffective in this. Aim at Heaven and you will get Earth "thrown in": aim at Earth and you will get neither. It seems a strange rule, but something like it can be seen at work in other matters. Health is a great blessing, but the moment you make health one of your main, direct objects you start becoming a crank and imagining there is something wrong with you. You are only likely to get health provided you want other things more— food, games, work, fun, open air. In the same way, we shall never save civilization as long as civilization is our main object. We must learn to want something else more.

Most of us find it very difficult to want "Heaven" at all— except insofar as "Heaven" means meeting again our friends who have died. One reason for this difficulty is that we have not been trained: our whole education tends to fix our minds on this world. Another reason is that when the real want for Heaven is present in us, we do not recognize it. Most people, if they had really learned to look into their own hearts, would know that they do want, and want acutely, something that cannot be had in this world. There are all sorts of things in this world that offer to give it to you, but they never quite keep their promise. The longings which arise in us when we first fall in love, or first think of some foreign country, or first take up some subject that excites us, are longings which no marriage, no travel, no learning, can really satisfy. I am not now speaking of what would ordinarily be called unsuccessful marriages, or holidays, or learned careers. I am speaking of the best possible ones. There was something we grasped at, in that first moment of longing, which just fades away in reality. I think everyone knows what I mean. The wife may be a good wife, and the hotels and scenery may have been excellent, and chemistry may be a very interesting job: but something has evaded us.

Charity

NATURAL LIKING OR AFFECTION for people makes it easier to be "charitable" toward them. It is, therefore, normally a duty to encourage our affections—to "like" people as much as we can (just as it is often our duty to encourage our liking for exercise or wholesome food)—not because this liking is itself the virtue of charity, but because it is a help to it. On the other hand, it is also necessary to keep a very sharp lookout for fear our liking for some one person makes us uncharitable, or even unfair, to someone else. There are even cases where our liking conflicts with our charity toward the person we like. For example, a doting mother may be tempted by natural affection to "spoil" her child; that is, to gratify her own affectionate impulses at the expense of the child's real happiness later on.

But though natural likings should normally be encouraged, it would be quite wrong to think that the way to become charitable is to sit trying to manufacture affectionate feelings. Some people are "cold" by temperament; that may be a misfortune for them, but it is no more a sin than having a bad digestion is a sin; and it does not cut them out from the chance, or excuse them from the duty, of learning charity. The rule for all of us is perfectly simple. Do not waste time bothering whether you "love" your neighbor; act as if you did. As soon as we do this, we find one of the great secrets. When you are behaving as if you loved someone, you will presently come to love him. If you injure someone you dislike, you will find yourself disliking him more. If you do him a good turn, you will find yourself disliking him less. There is, indeed, one exception. If you do him a good turn, not to please God and obey the law of charity, but to show him what a fine forgiving chap you are, and to put him in your debt, and then sit down to wait for his "gratitude," you will probably be disappointed. (People are not fools: they have a very quick eye for anything like showing off, or patronage.) But whenever we do good to another self, just because it is a self, made (like us) by God, and desiring its own happiness as we desire ours, we shall have learned to love it a little more or, at least, to dislike it less.

Consequently, though Christian charity sounds a very cold thing to people whose heads are full of sentimentality, and though it is quite distinct from affection, yet it leads to affection. The difference between a Christian and a worldly man is not that the worldly man has only affections or "likings" and the Christian has only "charity." The worldly man treats certain people kindly because he "likes" them:

the Christian, trying to treat everyone kindly, finds himself liking more and more people as he goes on—including people he could not even have imagined himself liking at the beginning.

Humility

IF ANYONE WOULD LIKE to acquire humility, I can, I think, tell him the first step. The first step is to realize that one is proud. And a biggish step, too. At least, nothing whatever can be done before it. If you think you are not conceited, it means you are very conceited indeed.

Forgiveness

EVERYONE SAYS FORGIVENESS is a lovely idea, until they have something to forgive, as we had during the war. And then to mention the subject at all is to be greeted with howls of anger. It is not that people think this too high and difficult a virtue: it is that they think it hateful and contemptible. "That sort of talk makes them sick," they say. And half of you already want to ask me, "I wonder how'd you feel about forgiving the Gestapo if you were a Pole or a Jew?"

So do I. I wonder very much. Just as when Christianity tells me that I must not deny my religion even to save myself from death by torture, I wonder very much what I should do when it came to the point. I am not trying to tell you . . . what I could do—I can do precious little—I am telling you what Christianity is. I did not invent it. And there, right in the middle of it, I find "Forgive us our sins as we forgive those that sin against us." There is no slightest suggestion that we are offered forgiveness on any other terms. It is made perfectly clear that if we do not forgive we shall not be forgiven. There are no two ways about it. What are we to do?

It is going to be hard enough, anyway, but I think there are two things we can do to make it easier. When you start mathematics you do not begin with calculus; you begin with simple addition. In the same way, if we really want (but all depends on really wanting) to learn how to forgive, perhaps we had better start with something easier than the Gestapo. One might start with forgiving one's husband or wife, or parents or children, or the nearest N.C.O., for something they have done or said in the last week. That will probably keep us busy for the moment. And secondly, we might try to understand exactly what loving your neighbor as yourself means. I have to love him as I love myself. Well, how exactly do I love myself?

Now that I come to think of it, I have not exactly got a feeling of fondness or affection for myself, and I do not even always enjoy my own society. So apparently "Love your neighbor" does not mean "feel fond of him" or "find him attractive." I ought to have seen that before, because, of course, you cannot feel fond of a person by trying. Do I think well of myself, think myself a nice chap? Well, I am afraid I sometimes do (and those are, no doubt, my worst moments) but that is not why I love myself. In fact it is the other way round: my self-love makes me think myself nice, but thinking myself nice is not why I love myself. So loving my enemies does not apparently mean thinking them nice either. That is an enormous relief. For a good many people imagine that forgiving your enemies means making out that they are really not such bad fellows after all, when it is quite plain that they are. Go a step further. In my most clear-sighted moments not only do I not think myself a nice

man, but I know that I am a very nasty one. I can look at
some of the things I have done with loathing and horror. So
apparently I am allowed to loathe and hate some of the
things my enemies do. Now that I come to think of it, I
remember Christian teachers telling me long ago that I must
hate a bad man's actions, but not hate the bad man: or, as
they would say, hate the sin but not the sinner.

For a long time I used to think this a silly, straw-splitting
distinction: how could you hate what a man did and not
hate the man? But years later it occurred to me that there
was one man to whom I had been doing this all my life—
namely myself. However much I might dislike my own
cowardice or conceit or greed, I went on loving myself.
There had never been the slightest difficulty about it. In
fact, the very reason why I hated the things was that I loved
the man. Just because I loved myself, I was sorry to find that
I was the sort of man who did those things. Consequently
Christianity does not want us to reduce by one atom the
hatred we feel for cruelty and treachery. We ought to hate
them. Not one word of what we have said about them
needs to be unsaid. But it does want us to hate them in the
same way in which we hate things in ourselves: being sorry
that the man should have done such things, and hoping, if
it is anyway possible, that somehow, sometime, somewhere, he can be cured and made human again.

Almsgiving

IN THE PASSAGE where the New Testament says that everyone must work, it gives as a reason "in order that he may
have something to give to those in need." Charity—giving
to the poor—is an essential part of Christian morality: in
the frightening parable of the sheep and the goats it seems

to be the point on which everything turns. Some people nowadays say that charity ought to be unnecessary and that instead of giving to the poor we ought to be producing a society in which there were no poor to give to. They may be quite right in saying we ought to produce that kind of society. But if anyone thinks that, as a consequence, you can stop giving in the meantime, then he has parted company with all Christian morality. I do not believe one can settle how much we ought to give. I am afraid the only safe rule is to give more than we can spare. In other words, if our expenditure on comforts, luxuries, amusements, etc., is up to the standard common among those with the same income as our own, we are probably giving away too little. If our charities do not at all pinch or hamper us, I should say they are too small. There ought to be things we should like to do and cannot do because our charitable expenditure excludes them. I am speaking now of "charities" in the common way. Particular cases of distress among your own relatives, friends, neighbors, or employees, which God, as it were, forces upon your notice, may demand much more: even to the crippling and endangering of your own position. For many of us the great obstacle to charity lies not in our luxurious living or desire for more money, but in our fear—fear of insecurity. This must often be recognized as a temptation. Sometimes our pride also hinders our charity; we are tempted to spend more than we ought on the showy forms of generosity (tipping, hospitality) and less than we ought on those who really need our help.

Obedience

NEARLY EVERYONE will find himself in the course of his life in positions where he ought to command and in positions where he ought to obey. . . . Now each of them requires a certain training or habituation if it is to be done well; and indeed the habit of command or of obedience may often be more necessary than the most enlightened views on the ultimate moral grounds for doing either. You can't begin training a child to command until it has reason and age enough to command someone or something without absurdity. You can at once begin training it to obey; that is, teaching it the art of obedience *as such*—without prejudice to the views it will hold later on as to who should obey whom, or when, or how much . . . since it is perfectly obvious that every human being is going to spend a great deal of his life in obeying.

The Devil

THE COMMONEST QUESTION [I am asked about *The Screwtape Letters*] is whether I really "believe in the Devil."

Now, if by "the Devil" you mean a power opposite to God and, like God, self-existent from all eternity, the answer is certainly No. There is no uncreated being except God. God has no opposite. No being could attain a "perfect badness" opposite to the perfect goodness of God; for when you have taken away every kind of good thing (intelligence, will, memory, energy, and existence itself), there would be none of him left.

The proper question is whether I believe in devils. I do. That is to say, I believe in angels, and I believe that some of these, by the abuse of their free will, have become enemies to God and, as a corollary, to us. These we may call devils. They do not differ in nature from good angels, but their nature is depraved. *Devil* is the opposite of *angel* only as Bad

Man is the opposite of Good Man. Satan, the leader or dictator of devils, is the opposite, not of God, but of Michael.

I believe this not in the sense that it is part of my creed, but in the sense that it is one of my opinions. My religion would not be in ruins if this opinion were shown to be false. Till that happens—and proofs of a negative are hard to come by—I shall retain it. It seems to me to explain a good many facts. It agrees with the plain sense of Scripture, the tradition of Christendom, and the beliefs of most men at most times. And it conflicts with nothing that any of the sciences has shown to be true.

Screwtape to Wormwood on Prayer

THE BEST THING, where it is possible, is to keep the patient from the serious intention of praying altogether. When the patient is an adult recently reconverted to the Enemy's party, like your man, this is best done by encouraging him to remember, or to think he remembers, the parrotlike nature of his prayers in childhood. In reaction against that, he may be persuaded to aim at something entirely spontaneous, inward, informal, and unregularized; and what this will actually mean to a beginner will be an effort to produce in himself a vaguely devotional *mood* in which real concentration of will and intelligence have no part. One of their poets, Coleridge, has recorded that he did not pray "with moving lips and bended knees" but merely "composed his spirit to love" and indulged "a sense of supplication." That is exactly the sort of prayer we want; and since it bears a superficial resemblance to the prayer of silence as practiced by those who are very far advanced in the Enemy's service, clever and lazy patients can be taken in by it for quite a long time. At the very least, they can be persuaded that the bodily position makes no difference to their prayers; for they constantly forget, what you must always remember, that they are animals and that whatever their bodies do affects their souls. It is funny how mortals always picture us as putting things into their minds: in reality our best work is done by keeping things out.

If this fails, you must fall back on a subtler misdirection of his intention. Whenever they are attending to the Enemy Himself we are defeated, but there are ways of preventing them from doing so. The simplest is to turn their gaze away from Him toward themselves. Keep them watching their own minds and trying to produce *feelings* there by the action of their own wills. When they meant to ask Him for charity, let them, instead, start trying to manufacture charitable feelings for themselves and not notice that this is what they are doing. When they meant to pray for courage, let them really be trying to feel brave. When they say they are praying for forgiveness, let them be trying to feel forgiven. Teach them to estimate the value of each prayer by their success in producing the desired feeling; and never let them suspect how much success or failure of that kind depends on whether they are well or ill, fresh or tired, at the moment.

Screwtape to Wormwood on War

WAR IS ENTERTAINING. The immediate fear and suffering of the humans is a legitimate and pleasing refreshment for our myriads of toiling workers. But what permanent good does it do us unless we make use of it for bringing souls to Our Father Below? When I see the temporal suffering of humans who finally escape us, I feel as if I had been allowed to taste the first course of a rich banquet and then denied the rest. It is worse than not to have tasted it at all. The Enemy, true to His barbarous methods of warfare, allows us to see the short misery of his favorites only to tantalize and torment us—to mock the incessant hunger which, during this present phase of the great conflict, His blockade is admittedly imposing. Let us therefore think rather how to use, than how to enjoy, this European war. For it has certain tendencies inherent in it which are, in themselves, by no means in our favor. We may hope for a good deal of cruelty and unchastity. But, if we are not careful, we shall see thousands turning in this tribulation to the Enemy, while tens of thousands who do not go so far as that will nevertheless have their attention diverted from themselves to values and causes which they believe to be higher than the self. I know that the Enemy disapproves many of these causes. But that is where He is so unfair. He often makes prizes of humans who have given their lives for causes He thinks bad on the monstrously sophistical ground that the humans thought them good and were following the best they knew. Consider too what undesirable deaths occur in wartime. Men are killed in places where they knew they might be killed and to which they go, if they are at all of the Enemy's party, prepared. How much better for us if *all* humans died in costly nursing homes amid doctors who lie, nurses who lie, as we have trained them, promising life to the dying, encouraging the belief that sickness excuses every indulgence, and even, if our workers know their job, withholding all suggestions of a priest lest it should betray to the sick man his true condition! And how disastrous for us is the continual remembrance of death which war enforces. One of our best weapons, contented worldliness, is rendered useless. In wartime not even a human can believe that he is going to live forever.

Screwtape to Wormwood on Anxiety

THERE IS NOTHING like suspense and anxiety for barricading a human's mind against the Enemy. He wants men to be concerned with what they do; our business is to keep them thinking about what will happen to them.

Your patient will, of course, have picked up the notion that he must submit with patience to the Enemy's will. What the Enemy means by this is primarily that he should accept with patience the tribulation which has actually been dealt out to him—the present anxiety and suspense. It is about *this* that he is to say "Thy will be done," and for the daily task of bearing *this* that the daily bread will be provided. It is your business to see that the patient never thinks of the present fear as his appointed cross, but only of the things he is afraid of. Let him regard them as his crosses: let him forget that, since they are incompatible, they cannot all happen to him, and let him try to practice fortitude and patience to them in advance. For real resignation, at the same moment, to a dozen different and hypothetical fates, is almost impossible, and the Enemy does not greatly assist those who are trying to attain it: resignation to present and actual suffering, even where that suffering consists of fear, is far easier, and is usually helped by this direct action.

Screwtape to Wormwood on Peaks and Troughs

HAS NO ONE ever told you about the law of Undulation?

Humans are amphibians—half spirit and half animal. (The Enemy's determination to produce such a revolting hybrid was one of the things that determined Our Father to withdraw his support from Him.) As spirits they belong to the eternal world, but as animals they inhabit time. This means that while their spirit can be directed to an eternal object, their bodies, passions, and imaginations are in continual change, for to be in time means to change. Their nearest approach to constancy, therefore, is undulation— the repeated return to a level from which they repeatedly fall back, a series of Troughs and Peaks. If you had watched your patient carefully, you would have seen this undulation in every department of his life—his interest in his work, his affection for his friends, his physical appetites, all go up and down. As long as he lives on earth, periods of emotional and bodily richness and liveliness will alternate with periods of numbness and poverty. The dryness and dullness through which your patient is now going are not, as you fondly suppose, your workmanship; they are merely a natural phenomenon which will do us no good unless you make a good use of it.

Screwtape to Wormwood on Lust

I HAVE ALWAYS found that the Trough periods of the human undulation provide excellent opportunity for all sensual temptations, particularly those of sex. This may surprise you, because, of course, there is more physical energy, and therefore more potential appetite, at the Peak periods; but you must remember that the powers of resistance are then also at their highest. The health and spirits which you want to use in producing lust can also, alas, be very easily used for work or play or thought or innocuous merriment. The attack has a much better chance of success when the man's whole inner world is drab and cold and empty. And it is also to be noted that the Trough sexuality is subtly different in quality from that of the Peak—much less likely to lead to the milk-and-water phenomenon which the humans call "being in love," much more easily drawn into perversions, much less contaminated by those generous and imaginative and even spiritual concomitants which often render human sexuality so disappointing. It is the same with other desires of the flesh. You are much more likely to make your man a sound drunkard by pressing drink on him as an anodyne when he is dull and weary than by encouraging him to use it as a means of merriment among his friends when he is happy and expansive. Never forget that when we are dealing with any pleasure in its healthy and normal and satisfying form, we are, in a sense, on the Enemy's ground. I know we have won many a soul through pleasure. All the same, it is His invention, not ours. He made the pleasures:

all our research so far has not enabled us to produce one. All we can do is to encourage the humans to take the pleasures which our Enemy has produced, at times, or in ways, or in degrees, which He has forbidden. Hence we always try to work away from the natural condition of any pleasure to that in which it is least natural, least redolent of its Maker, and least pleasurable. An ever increasing craving for an ever diminishing pleasure is the formula. It is more certain; and it's better *style*. To get the man's soul and give him *nothing* in return—that is what really gladdens Our Father's heart. And the Troughs are the time for beginning the process.

Screwtape to Wormwood on Worldly Companions

I WAS DELIGHTED to hear . . . that your patient has made some very desirable new acquaintances and that you seem to have used this event in a really promising manner. I gather that the middle-aged couple who called at his office are just the sort of people we want him to know—rich, smart, superficially intellectual, and brightly skeptical about everything in the world. I gather they are even vaguely pacifist, not on moral grounds but from an ingrained habit of belittling anything that concerns the great mass of their fellow men and from a dash of purely fashionable and literary communism. This is excellent. And you seem to have made good use of all his social, sexual, and intellectual vanity. Tell me more. Did he commit himself deeply? I don't mean in words. There is a subtle play of looks and tones and laughs by which a mortal can imply that he is of the same party as those to whom he is speaking. That is the kind of betrayal you should specially encourage, because the man does not fully realize it himself; and by the time he does you will have made withdrawal difficult.

No doubt he must very soon realize that his own faith is in direct opposition to the assumptions on which all the conversation of his new friends is based. I don't think that matters much, provided that you can persuade him to postpone any open acknowledgment of the fact, and this, with the aid of shame, pride, modesty, and vanity, will be easy to do. As long as the postponement lasts, he will be in a false position. He will be silent when he ought to speak and laugh when he ought to be silent. He will assume, at first only by his manner, but presently by his words, all sorts of cynical and skeptical attitudes which are not really his. But if you play him well, they may become his. All mortals tend to turn into the thing they are pretending to be. This is elementary. The real question is how to prepare for the Enemy's counterattack.

Screwtape to Wormwood on Humility

YOUR PATIENT has become humble; have you drawn his attention to the fact? All virtues are less formidable to us once the man is aware that he has them, but this is specially true of humility. Catch him at the moment when he is really poor in spirit and smuggle into his mind the gratifying reflection, "By jove! I'm being humble," and almost immediately pride—pride at his own humility—will appear. If he awakes to the danger and tries to smother this new form of pride, make him proud of his attempt—and so on, through as many stages as you please. But don't try this too long, for fear you awake his sense of humor and proportion, in which case he will merely laugh at you and go to bed.

But there are other profitable ways of fixing his attention on the virtue of Humility. By this virtue, as by all the others, our Enemy want to turn the man's attention away from self to Him, and to the man's neighbors. All the abjection and self-hatred are designed, in the long run, solely for this end; unless they attain this end they do us little harm; and they may even do us good if they keep the man concerned with himself, and, above all, if self-contempt can be made the starting point for contempt of other selves, and thus for gloom, cynicism, and cruelty.

You must therefore conceal from the patient the true end of Humility. Let him think of it, not as self-forgetfulness, but as a certain kind of opinion (namely, a low opinion) of his own talents and character. Some talents, I gather, he really has. Fix in his mind the idea that humility consists in trying to believe those talents to be less valuable than he believes them to be. No doubt they *are* in fact less valuable than he believes, but that is not the point. The great thing is to make him value an opinion for some quality other than truth, thus introducing an element of dishonesty and make-believe into the heart of what otherwise threatens to become a virtue. By this method thousands of humans have been brought to think that humility means pretty women trying to believe they are ugly and clever men trying to believe they are fools. And since what they are trying to believe may, in some cases, be manifest nonsense, they cannot succeed in believing it, and we have the chance of keeping their minds endlessly revolving on themselves in an effort to achieve the impossible.

Screwtape to Wormwood on Laughter

I DIVIDE THE CAUSES of human laughter into Joy, Fun, the Joke Proper, and Flippancy. You will see the first among friends and lovers reunited on the eve of a holiday. Among adults some pretext in the way of Jokes is usually provided, but the facility with which the smallest witticisms produce laughter at such a time shows that they are not the real cause. What that real cause is we do not know. Something like it is expressed in much of that detestable art which the humans call Music, and something like it occurs in Heaven—a meaningless acceleration in the rhythm of celestial experience, quite opaque to us. Laughter of this kind does us no good and should always be discouraged. Besides, the phenomenon is of itself disgusting and a direct insult to the realism, dignity, and austerity of Hell.

Fun is closely related to Joy—a sort of emotional froth arising from the play instinct. It is very little use to us. It can sometimes be used, of course, to divert humans from something else which the Enemy would like them to be feeling or doing: but in itself it has wholly undesirable tendencies; it promotes charity, courage, contentment, and many other evils.

The Joke Proper, which turns on sudden perception of incongruity, is a much more promising field. I am not thinking primarily of indecent or bawdy humor, which, though much relied upon by second-rate tempters, is often disappointing in its results. The truth is that humans are pretty clearly divided on this matter into two classes. There are some to whom "no passion is as serious as lust" and for whom an indecent story ceases to produce lasciviousness precisely insofar as it becomes funny: there are others in whom laughter and lust are excited at the same moment and by the same things. The first sort joke about sex because it gives rise to many incongruities; the second cultivate incongruities because they afford a pretext for talking about sex. If your man is of the first type, bawdy humor will not help you—I shall never forget the hours which I wasted (hours to me of unbearable tedium) with one of my early patients in bars and smoking rooms before I learned this rule. Find out which group the patient belongs to—and see that he does *not* find out.

The real use of Jokes or Humor is in quite a different direction, and it is especially promising among the English, who take their "sense of humor" so seriously that a deficiency in this sense is almost the only deficiency at which they feel shame. Humor is for them the all-consoling and (mark this) the all-excusing, grace of life. Hence it is invaluable as a means of destroying shame. If a man simply lets others pay for him, he is "mean"; if he boasts of it in a jocular manner and twits his fellows with having been scored off, he is no longer "mean" but a comical fellow. Mere cowardice is shameful; cowardice boasted of with humorous exaggerations and grotesque gestures can be passed off as funny. Cruelty is shameful—unless the cruel man can represent it as a practical joke. A thousand bawdy, or even blasphemous, jokes do not help toward a man's damnation so much as his discovery that almost anything he wants to do can be done, not only without the disapproval but with the admiration of his fellows, if only it can get itself treated as a Joke. And this temptation can be almost entirely hidden from your patient by that English seriousness about Humor. Any suggestion that there might be too much of it can be represented to him as "Puritanical" or as betraying a "lack of humor."

But Flippancy is the best of all. In the first place it is very economical. Only a clever human can make a real Joke about virtue, or indeed about anything else; any of them can be trained to talk *as if* virtue were funny. Among flippant people the Joke is always assumed to have been made. No one actually makes it; but every serious subject is discussed in a manner which implies that they have already found a ridiculous side to it. If prolonged, the habit of Flippancy builds up around a man the finest armor plating against the Enemy that I know, and it is quite free from the dangers inherent in the other sources of laughter. It is a thousand miles away from joy; it deadens, instead of sharpening, the intellect; and it excites no affection between those who practice it.

Screwtape to Wormwood on Irregular Churchgoing

IF A MAN can't be cured of churchgoing, the next best thing is to send him all over the neighborhood looking for the church that "suits" him until be becomes a taster or connoisseur of churches.

The reasons are obvious. In the first place, the parochial organization should always be attacked, because, being a unity of place and not of likings, it brings people of different classes and psychology together in the kind of unity the Enemy desires. The congregational principle, on the other hand, makes each church into a kind of club, and finally, if all goes well, into a coterie or faction. In the second place, the search for a "suitable" church makes the man a critic where the Enemy wants him to be a pupil. What He wants of the layman in church is an attitude which may, indeed, be critical in the sense of rejecting what is false or unhelpful, but which is wholly uncritical in the sense that it does not appraise—does not waste time in thinking about what it rejects, but lays itself open in uncommenting, humble receptivity to any nourishment that is going. (You see how groveling, how unspiritual, how irredeemably vulgar He is!) This attitude, especially during sermons, creates the condition (most hostile to our whole policy) in which platitudes can become really audible to a human soul. There is hardly any sermon, or any book, which may not be dangerous to us if it is received in this temper. So pray bestir yourself and send this fool the round of the neighboring churches as soon as possible.

Screwtape to Wormwood on Gluttony

ONE OF THE GREAT achievements of the last hundred years has been to deaden the human conscience on [gluttony], so that by now you will hardly find a sermon preached or a conscience troubled about it in the whole length and breadth of Europe. This has largely been effected by concentrating all our efforts on gluttony of Delicacy, not gluttony of Excess. Your patient's mother, as I learn from the dossier . . . is a good example. She would be astonished— one day, I hope, *will* be—to learn that her whole life is enslaved to this kind of sensuality, which is quite concealed from her by the fact that the quantities involved are small. But what do the quantities matter, provided we can use a human belly and palate to produce querulousness, impa-

tience, uncharitableness, and self-concern? . . . She is a
positive terror to hostesses and servants. She is always
turning from what has been offered her to say with a de-
mure little sigh and a smile, "Oh, please, please . . . *all* I
want is a cup of tea, weak but not too weak, and the tee-
niest-weeniest bit of really crisp toast." You see? Because
what she wants is smaller and less costly than what has
been set before her, she never recognizes as gluttony her
determination to get what she wants, however troublesome
it may be to others. At the very moment of indulging her
appetite she believes that she is practicing temperance. In a
crowded restaurant she gives a little scream at the plate
which some overworked waitress has set before her and
says: "Oh, that's far, far too much! Take it away and bring
me about a quarter of it." If challenged, she would say she
was doing this to avoid waste; in reality she does it because
the particular shade of delicacy to which we have enslaved
her is offended by the sight of more food than she happens
to want.

Screwtape to Wormwood on Reinterpreting Jesus

A GOOD MANY Christian-political writers think that
Christianity began going wrong, and departing from the
doctrine of its Founder, at a very early stage. Now this idea
must be used by us to encourage once again the conception
of a "historical Jesus" to be found by clearing away later
"accretions and perversions" and then to be contrasted with
the whole Christian tradition. In the last generation we pro-
moted the construction of such a "historical Jesus" on lib-

eral and humanitarian lines; we are now putting forward a
new "historical Jesus" on Marxian, catastrophic, and revo-
lutionary lines. The advantages of these constructions,
which we intend to change every thirty years or so, are
manifold.

In the first place, they all tend to direct men's devotion to
something which does not exist, for each "historical Jesus"
is unhistorical. The documents say what they say and cannot be added to; each new "historical Jesus" therefore has
to be got out of them by suppression at one point and exag-
geration at another, and by that sort of guessing (*brilliant* is
the adjective we teach humans to apply to it) on which no
one would risk ten shillings in ordinary life, but which is
enough to produce a crop of new Napoleons, new Shake-
speares, and new Swifts in every publisher's autumn list.

In the second place, all such constructions place the importance of their "historical Jesus" in some peculiar theory
He is supposed to have promulgated. He has to be a "great
man" in the modern sense of the word—one standing at the
terminus of some centrifugal and unbalanced line of
thought—a crank vending a panacea. We thus distract
men's minds from Who He is, and what He did. We first
make Him solely a teacher, and then conceal the very sub-
stantial agreement between His teachings and those of all
other great moral teachers. For humans must not be allowed
to notice that all great moralists are sent by the Enemy, not
to inform men, but to remind them, to restate the primeval
moral platitudes against our continual concealment of them.
We make the Sophists: He raises up a Socrates to answer
them.

Our third aim is, by these constructions, to destroy the
devotional life. For the real presence of the Enemy, otherwise experienced by men in prayer and sacrament, we substitute a merely probable, remote, shadowy, and uncouth
figure, one who spoke a strange language and died a long
time ago. Such an object cannot, in fact, be worshiped. In-

stead of the Creator adored by the creature, you soon have merely a leader acclaimed by a partisan, and finally a distinguished character approved by a judicious historian.

And fourthly, beside being unhistorical in the Jesus it depicts, religion of this kind is false to history in another sense. No nation, and few individuals, are really brought into the Enemy's camp by the historical study of the biography of Jesus, simply as biography. Indeed, materials for a full biography have been withheld from men. The earliest converts were converted by a single historical fact (the Resurrection) and a single theological doctrine (the Redemption) operating on a sense of sin which they already had— and sin, not against some new fancy dress law produced as a novelty by a "great man," but against the old, platitudinous, universal moral law which they had been taught by their nurses and mothers. The "Gospels" come later, and were written, not to make Christians, but to edify Christians already made.

The "historical Jesus," then, however dangerous he may seem to be to us at some particular point, is always to be encouraged. About the general connection between Christianity and politics, our position is more delicate. Certainly we do not want men to allow their Christianity to flow over into their political life, for the establishment of anything like a really just society would be a major disaster. On the other hand we do want, and want very much, to make men treat Christianity as a means; preferably, of course, as a means to their own advancement, but, failing that, as a means to anything—even to social justice. The thing to do is to get a man at first to value social justice as a thing which the Enemy demands, and then work him on to the stage at which he values Christianity because it may produce social justice. For the Enemy will not be used as a convenience. Men or nations who think they can revive the Faith in order to make a good society might just as well think they can use the stairs of Heaven as a shortcut to the nearest chemist's shop. Fortunately it is quite easy to coax humans round this little corner. Only today I have found a passage in a Christian writer where he recommends his own version of Christianity on the ground that "only such a faith can outlast the death of old cultures and the birth of new civilizations." You see the little rift? "Believe this, not because it is true, but for some other reason." That's the game.

Everythingism

I MEAN BY *Everythingism* the belief that "everything," or "the whole show," must be self-existent, must be more important than every particular thing, and must contain all particular things in such a way that they cannot be really very different from one another—that they must be not merely "at one," but one. Thus the Everythingist, if he starts from God, becomes a Pantheist; there must be nothing that is not God. If he starts from Nature he becomes a Naturalist; there must be nothing that is not Nature. He thinks that everything is in the long run "merely" a precursor or a development or a relic or an instance or a disguise, of everything else. This philosophy I believe to be profoundly untrue. One of the moderns has said that reality is "incorrigibly plural." I think he is right. All things come from One. All things are related—related in different and complicated ways. But all things are not one. The word "everything" should mean simply the total (a total to be reached, if we knew enough, by enumeration) of all the things that exist at a given moment. It must not be given a mental capital letter; must not (under the influence of picture thinking) be turned into a sort of pool in which particular things sink or even a cake in which they are the currants. Real things are sharp and knobbly and complicated and different. Everythingism is congenial to our minds because it is the natural philosophy of a totalitarian, mass-producing, conscripted age. That is why we must be perpetually on our guard against it.

Sins of Thought

[CHRISTIAN WRITERS] seem to be so very strict at one moment and so very free and easy at another. They talk about mere sins of thought as if they were immensely important: and then they talk about the most frightful murders and treacheries as if you had only got to repent and all would be forgiven. But I have come to see that they are right. What they are always thinking of is the mark which the action leaves on that tiny central self which no one sees in this life but which each of us will have to endure—or—enjoy—forever. One man may be so placed that his anger sheds the blood of thousands, and another so placed that however angry he gets he will only be laughed at. But the little mark on the soul may be much the same in both. Each has done something to himself which, unless he repents, will make it harder for him to keep out of the rage next time he is tempted, and will make the rage worse when he does fall into it. Each of them, if he seriously turns to God, can have that twist in the central man straightened out again: each is, in the long run, doomed if he will not. The bigness or smallness of the thing, seen from the outside, is not what really matters.

Pride

ACCORDING TO Christian teachers, the essential vice, the utmost evil, is Pride. Unchastity, anger, greed, drunkenness, and all that, are mere fleabites in comparison: it was through Pride that the devil became the devil: Pride leads to every other vice: it is the complete anti-God state of mind.

Does this seem exaggerated? If so, think it over. I pointed out a moment ago that the more pride one had, the more one disliked pride in others. In fact, if you want to find out how proud you are, the easiest way is to ask yourself, "How much do I dislike it when other people snub me, or refuse to take any notice of me, or shove their oar in, or patronize me, or show off?" The point is that each person's pride is in competition with everyone else's pride. It is because I wanted to be the big noise at the party that I am so annoyed at someone else being the big noise. Two of a trade never agree. Now what you want to get clear is that Pride is *essentially* competitive—is competitive by its very nature—while the other vices are competitive only, so to speak, by accident. Pride gets no pleasure out of having something, only out of having more of it than the next man. We say that people are proud of being rich, or clever, or good-looking, but they are not. They are proud of being richer, or cleverer, or better-looking than others. If everyone else became equally rich, or clever, or good-looking, there would be nothing to be proud about. It is the comparison that makes you proud: the pleasure of being above the rest. Once the element of competition has gone, pride has gone. That is why I say that Pride is essentially competitive in a

way the other vices are not. The sexual impulse may drive
two men into competition if they both want the same girl.
But that is only by accident; they might just as likely have
wanted two different girls. But a proud man will take your
girl from you, not because he wants her, but just to prove to
himself that he is a better man than you. Greed may drive
men into competition if there is not enough to go round;
but the proud man, even when he has got more than he can
possibly want, will try to get still more just to assert his
power. Nearly all those evils in the world which people put
down to greed or selfishness are really far more the result of
Pride.

Take it with money. Greed will certainly make a man
want money, for the sake of a better house, better holidays,
better things to eat and drink. But only up to a point. What
is it that makes a man with £10,000 a year anxious to get
£20,000 a year? It is not the greed for more pleasure. £10,000
will give all the luxuries that any man can really enjoy. It is
Pride—the wish to be richer than some other rich man, and
(still more) the wish for power. For, of course, power is
what Pride really enjoys: there is nothing makes a man feel
so superior to others as being able to move them about like
toy soldiers. What makes a pretty girl spread misery wherever she goes by collecting admirers? Certainly not her sexual instinct: that kind of girl is quite often sexually frigid. It
is Pride. What is it that makes a political leader or a whole
nation go on and on, demanding more and more? Pride
again. Pride is competitive by its very nature: that is why it
goes on and on. If I am a proud man, then, as long as there
is one man in the whole world more powerful, or richer, or
cleverer than I, he is my rival and my enemy.

The Christians are right: it is Pride which has been the
chief cause of misery in every nation and every family since
the world began. Other vices may sometimes bring people
together: you may find good fellowship and jokes and

friendliness among drunken people or unchaste people. But Pride always means enmity—it *is* enmity. And not only enmity between man and man but enmity to God.

In God you come up against something which is in every respect immeasurably superior to yourself. Unless you know God as that—and, therefore, know yourself as nothing in comparison—you do not know God at all. As long as you are proud, you cannot know God. A proud man is always looking down on things and people: and, of course, as long as you are looking down, you cannot see something that is above you.

That raises a terrible question. How is it that people who are quite obviously eaten up with Pride can say they believe in God and appear to themselves very religious? I am afraid it means they are worshiping an imaginary God. They theoretically admit themselves to be nothing in the presence of this phantom God, but are really all the time imagining how He approves of them and thinks them far better than ordinary people: that is, they pay a pennyworth of imaginary humility to Him and get out of it a pound's worth of Pride toward their fellowmen. I suppose it was of those people Christ was thinking when He said that some would preach about Him and cast out devils in His name, only to be told at the end of the world that He had never known them. And any of us may at any moment be in this deathtrap. Luckily, we have a test. Whenever we find that our religious life is making us feel that we are good—above all, that we are better than someone else—I think we may be sure that we are being acted on, not by God, but by the devil. The real test of being in the presence of God is that you either forget about yourself altogether or see yourself as a small, dirty object. It is better to forget about yourself altogether.

It is a terrible thing that the worst of all the vices can smuggle itself into the very center of our religious life. But you can see why. The other, and less bad, vices come from the devil working on us through our animal nature. But this does not come through our animal nature at all. It comes direct from Hell. It is purely spiritual: consequently it is far more subtle and deadly. For the same reason, Pride can often be used to beat down the simpler vices. Teachers, in fact, often appeal to a boy's Pride, or, as they call it, his self-respect, to make him behave decently: many a man has overcome cowardice, or lust, or ill temper by learning to think that they are beneath his dignity—that is, by Pride. The devil laughs. He is perfectly content to see you becoming chaste and brave and self-controlled provided, all the time, he is setting up in you the Dictatorship of Pride—just as he would be quite content to see your chilblains cured if he was allowed, in return, to give you cancer. For Pride is spiritual cancer: it eats up the very possibility of love, or contentment, or even common sense.

Human Wickedness

CHRIST TAKES IT for granted that men are bad. Until we really feel this assumption of His to be true, though we are part of the world He came to save, we are not part of the audience to whom His words are addressed. We lack the first condition for understanding what He is talking about. And when men attempt to be Christians without this preliminary consciousness of sin, the result is almost bound to be a certain resentment against God as to one who is always making impossible demands and always inexplicably angry. Most of us have at times felt a secret sympathy with the dying farmer who replied to the Vicar's dissertation on repentance by asking "What harm have I ever done *Him?*" There is the real rub. The worst we have done to God is to leave Him alone—why can't He return the compliment? Why not live and let live? What call has He, of all beings, to be "angry"? It's easy for Him to be good!

Now at the moment when a man feels real guilt—moments too rare in our lives—all these blasphemies vanish away. Much, we may feel, can be excused to human infirmities: but not *this*—this incredibly mean and ugly action which none of our friends would have done, which even such a thoroughgoing little rotter as X would have been ashamed of, which we would not for the world allow to be published. At such a moment we really do know that our character, as revealed in this action, is, and ought to be, hateful to all good men, and, if there are powers above man, to them. A God who did not regard this with unappeasable distaste would not be a good being. We cannot even wish for such a God—it is like wishing that every nose in the universe were abolished, that smell of hay, or roses, or the sea should never again delight any creature, because our own breath happens to stink.

When we merely *say* that we are bad, the "wrath" of God seems a barbarous doctrine; as soon as we *perceive* our badness, it appears inevitable, a mere corollary from God's goodness. To keep ever before us the insight derived from such a moment as I have been describing, to learn to detect the same real inexcusable corruption under more and more of its complex disguises, is therefore indispensable to a real understanding of the Christian faith. This is not, of course, a new doctrine. . . . I am merely trying to get my reader (and, still more, myself) over a *pons asinorum*—to take the first step out of fools' paradise and utter illusion.

Laziness

I HAVE RECENTLY come to the conclusion that a besetting sin of mine all my life has been one which I never suspected—laziness—and that a good deal of the high-sounding doctrine of leisure is only a defense of *that*. The Greek error was a punishment for their sin in owning slaves and their consequent contempt for labor. There was a good element in it—the recognition, badly needed by modern commercialism, that the economic activities are not the *end* of man: beyond that they were probably wrong. If I still wanted to defend my old view I should ask you why *toil* appears in Genesis not as one of the things God originally created and pronounced "very good" but as a punishment for sin, like death. I suppose one could point out in reply that Adam was a gardener before he was a sinner, and that we must distinguish two degrees and kinds of work—the one wholly good and necessary to the animal side of the *animal rationale,* the other a punitive deterioration of the former due to the Fall.

Guilt

MANY MODERN PSYCHOLOGISTS tell us always to distrust this vague feeling of guilt, as something purely pathological. And if they had stopped at that, I might believe them. But when they go on, as some do, to apply the same treatment to all guilt feelings whatever, to suggest that one's feeling about a particular unkind act or a particular insincerity is also and equally untrustworthy—I can't help thinking they are talking nonsense. One sees this the moment one looks at other people. I have talked to some who felt guilt when they jolly well ought to have felt it; they have behaved like brutes and know it. I've also met others who felt guilty and weren't guilty by any standard I can apply. And thirdly, I've met people who were guilty and didn't seem to feel guilt. And isn't this what we should expect? People can be *malades imaginaires* who are well and think they are ill; and others, especially consumptives, are ill and think they are well; and thirdly—far the largest class—people are ill and know they are ill. It would be very odd if there were any region in which all mistakes were in one direction.

Some Christians would tell us to go on rummaging and scratching till we find something specific. We may be sure, they say, that there are real sins enough to justify the guilt feeling or to overthrow the feeling that all is well. I think they are right in saying that if we hunt long enough we shall find, or think we have found, something. But that is just what wakens suspicion. A theory which could never by any experience be falsified can for that reason hardly be verified. And just as, when we are yielding to temptation, we make ourselves believe that what we have always thought sin will on this occasion, for some strange reason, not be a sin, shan't we persuade ourselves that something we have always (rightly) thought to be innocent was really wrong? We may create scruples. And scruples are always a bad thing—if only because they usually distract us from real duties.

I don't at all know whether I'm right or not, but I have, on the whole, come to the conclusion that one can't directly *do* anything about either feeling. One is not to believe either—indeed, how can one believe a fog? I come back to St. John: "if our heart condemn us, God is greater than our heart." I sometimes pray not for self-knowledge in general but for just so much self-knowledge at the moment as I can bear and use at the moment; the little daily dose.

Anxiety

SOME PEOPLE feel guilty about their anxieties and regard them as a defect of faith. I don't agree at all. They are afflictions, not sins. Like all afflictions, they are, if we can so take them, our share in the Passion of Christ. For the beginning of the Passion—the first move, so to speak—is in Gethsemane. In Gethsemane a very strange and significant thing seems to have happened.

It is clear from many of His sayings that Our Lord had long foreseen His death. He knew what conduct such as His, in a world such as we have made of this, must inevitably lead to. But it is clear that this knowledge must somehow have been withdrawn from Him before He prayed in Gethsemane. He could not, with whatever reservation about the Father's will, have prayed that the cup might pass and simultaneously known that it would not. That is both a logical and a psychological impossibility. You see what this involves? Lest any trial incident to humanity should be lacking, the torments of hope—of suspense, anxiety—were at the last moment loosed upon Him—the supposed possibility that, after all, He might, He just conceivably might, be spared the supreme horror. There was precedent. Isaac had been spared: he too at the last moment, he also against all apparent probability. It was not quite impossible . . . a sight very unlike most of our religious pictures and images.

But for this last (and erroneous) hope against hope, and the consequent tumult of the soul, the sweat of blood, perhaps He would not have been very Man. To live in a fully predictable world is not to be a man.

At the end, I know, we are told that an angel appeared "comforting" him. But neither *comforting* in . . . English nor . . . in Greek means "consoling." "Strengthening" is more the word. May not the strengthening have consisted in the renewed certainty—cold comfort this—that the thing must be endured and therefore could be?

We all try to accept with some sort of submission our afflictions when they actually arrive. But the prayer in Gethsemane shows that the preceding anxiety is equally God's will and equally part of our human destiny. The perfect Man experienced it. And the servant is not greater than the master. We are Christians, not Stoics.

Psychoanalysis

SINCE CHRISTIAN MORALITY claims to be a technique for putting the human machine right, I think you would like to know how it is related to another technique which seems to make a similar claim—namely, psychoanalysis.

Now you want to distinguish very clearly between two things: between the actual medical theories and technique of the psychoanalysts, and the general philosophical view of the world which Freud and some others have gone on to add to this. The second thing—the philosophy of Freud—is in direct contradiction to Christianity: and also in direct contradiction to the other great psychologist, Jung. And furthermore, when Freud is talking about how to cure neurotics, he is speaking as a specialist on his own subject, but when he goes on to talk general philosophy, he is speaking as an amateur. It is, therefore, quite sensible to attend to him with respect in the one case and not in the other—and that is what I do. I am all the readier to do it because I have found that, when he is talking off his own subject and on a subject I do know something about (namely, languages), he is very ignorant. But psychoanalysis itself, apart from all the philosophical additions that Freud and others have made to it, is not in the least contradictory to Christianity. Its technique overlaps with Christian morality at some points and it would not be a bad thing if every parson knew something about it: but it does not run the same course all the way, for the two techniques are doing rather different things.

When a man makes a moral choice, two things are involved. One is the act of choosing. The other is the various feelings, impulses and so on which his psychological outfit presents him with, and which are the raw material of his choice. Now this raw material may be of two kinds. Either it may be what we would call normal: it may consist of the sort of feelings that are common to all men. Or else it may consist of quite unnatural feelings due to things that have gone wrong in his subconscious. Thus fear of things that are really dangerous would be an example of the first kind: an irrational fear of cats or spiders would be an example of the second kind. The desire of a man for a woman would be of the first kind: the perverted desire of a man for a man would be of the second. Now what psychoanalysis undertakes to do is to remove the abnormal feelings, that is, to give the man better raw material for his acts of choice: morality is concerned with the acts of choice themselves.

Social Morality

THE FIRST THING to get clear about Christian morality between man and man is that in this department Christ did not come to preach any brand-new morality. The Golden

Rule of the New Testament (Do as you would be done by) is a summing up of what everyone, at bottom, had always known to be right. Really great moral teachers never do introduce new moralities: it is quacks and cranks who do that. As Dr. Johnson said, "People need to be reminded more often than they need to be instructed." The real job of every moral teacher is to keep on bringing us back, time after time, to the old simple principles which we are all so anxious not to see; like bringing a horse back and back to the fence it has refused to jump or bringing a child back and back to the bit in its lesson that it wants to shirk.

The second thing to get clear is that Christianity has not, and does not profess to have, a detailed program for applying "Do as you would be done by" to a particular society at a particular moment. It could not have. It is meant for all men at all times and the particular program which suited one place or time would not suit another. And, anyhow, that is not how Christianity works. When it tells you to feed the hungry, it does not give you lessons in cookery. When it tells you to read the Scriptures, it does not give you lessons in Hebrew and Greek, or even in English grammar. It was never intended to replace or supersede the ordinary human arts and sciences: it is rather a director which will set them all to the right jobs, and a source of energy which will give them all new life, if only they will put themselves at its disposal.

People say, "The Church ought to give us a lead." That is true if they mean it in the right way, but false if they mean it in the wrong way. By the Church they ought to mean the whole body of practicing Christians. And when they say that the Church should give us a lead, they ought to mean that some Christians—those who happen to have the right talents—should be economists and statesmen, and that all economists and statesmen should be Christians, and that their whole efforts in politics and economics should be directed to putting "Do as you would be done by" into action. If that happened, and if we others were really ready to take it, then we should find the Christian solution for our own social problems pretty quickly. But, of course, when they ask for a lead from the Church, most people mean they want the clergy to put out a political program. That is silly. The clergy are those particular people within the whole Church who have been specially trained and set aside to look after what concerns us as creatures who are going to live forever: and we are asking them to do a quite different job for which they have not been trained. The job is really on us, on the laymen. The application of Christian principles, say, to trade unionism or education, must come from Christian trade unionists and Christian schoolmasters: just as Christian literature comes from Christian novelists and dramatists—not from the bench of bishops getting together and trying to write plays and novels in their spare time.

Christian Society

THE NEW TESTAMENT, without going into details, gives us a pretty clear hint of what a fully Christian society would be like. Perhaps it gives us more than we can take. It tells us that there are to be no passengers or parasites: if a man does not work, he ought not to eat. Everyone is to work with his own hands, and what is more, everyone's work is to produce something good: there will be no manufacture of silly luxuries and then of sillier advertisements to persuade us to buy them. And there is to be no "swank" or "side," no putting on airs. To that extent a Christian society would be what we now call Leftist. On the other hand, it is always insisting on obedience—obedience (and outward marks of respect) from all of us to properly appointed magistrates, from children to parents, and (I am afraid this is going to be very unpopular) from wives to husbands. Thirdly, it is to be a cheerful society: full of singing and rejoicing, and regarding worry or anxiety as wrong. Courtesy is one of the Christian virtues; and the New Testament hates what it calls "busybodies."

If there were such a society in existence and you or I visited it, I think we should come away with a curious impression. We should feel that its economic life was very socialistic and, in that sense, "advanced," but that its family life and code of manners were rather old-fashioned—perhaps even ceremonious and aristocratic. Each of us would like some bits of it, but I'm afraid very few of us would like the whole thing. That is just what one would expect if Christianity is the total plan for the human machine. We have all departed from that total plan in different ways, and each of us wants to make out that his own modification of the original plan is the plan itself. You will find this again and again about anything that is really Christian: everyone is attracted by bits of it and wants to pick out those bits and leave the rest. That is why we do not get much further: and that is why people who are fighting for quite opposite things can both say they are fighting for Christianity.

Ecumenism

IT IS A LITTLE DIFFICULT to explain how I feel that though you have taken a way which is not for me [his correspondent had left the Episcopal Church to become a Roman Catholic], I nevertheless can congratulate you—I suppose because your faith and joy are so obviously increased. Naturally I do not draw the same conclusions as you—but there is no need for us to start a controversial correspondence! I believe we are very near to one another, but not because I am at all on the Romeward frontier of my own communion. I believe that, in the present divided state of Christendom, those who are at the heart of each division are all closer to one another than those who are at the fringes. I would even carry this beyond the borders of Christianity: how much more one has in common with a *real* Jew or Muslim than with a wretched liberalizing, occidentalized specimen of the same categories. Let us by all means pray for one another: it is perhaps the only form of "work for reunion" which never does anything but good. God bless you.

Other Religions

IF YOU ARE A CHRISTIAN, you do not have to believe that all the other religions are simply wrong all through. If you are an atheist, you do have to believe that the main point in all the religions of the whole world is simply one huge mistake. If you are a Christian, you are free to think that all these religions, even the queerest ones, contain at least some hint of the truth. When I was an atheist, I had to try to persuade myself that most of the human race have always been wrong about the question that mattered to them most; when I became a Christian, I was able to take a more liberal view. But, of course, being a Christian does mean thinking that where Christianity differs from other religions, Christianity is right and they are wrong. As in arithmetic—there is only one right answer to a sum, and all other answers are wrong: but some of the wrong answers are much nearer being right than others.

Fascism and Communism

FASCISM AND COMMUNISM, like all other evils, are potent because of the good they contain or imitate. . . . And of course their occasion is the failure of those who left humanity starved of that particular good. This does not for me alter the conviction that they are very bad indeed. One of the things we must guard against is the penetration of both into Christianity—availing themselves of that very truth you have suggested and I have admitted. Mark my words: you will presently see both a Leftist and a Rightist pseudo-theology developing—the abomination will stand where it ought not. . . .

Is Christianity Hard or Easy?

THE ORDINARY IDEA which we all have before we become Christians is this. We take as starting point our ordinary self with its various desires and interests. We then admit that something else—call it "morality" or "decent behavior," or "the good of society"—has claims on this self: claims which interfere with its own desires. What we mean by "being good" is giving in to those claims. Some of the things the ordinary self wanted to do turn out to be what we call "wrong": well, we must give them up. Other things, which the self did not want to do, turn out to be what we call "right": well, we shall have to do them. But we are hoping all the time that when all the demands have been met, the poor natural self will still have some chance, and some time, to get on with its own life and do what it likes. In fact, we are very like an honest man paying his taxes. He pays them all right, but he does hope that there will be enough left over for him to live on. Because we are still taking our natural self as the starting point.

As long as we are thinking that way, one or the other of two results is likely to follow. Either we give up trying to be good, or else we become very unhappy indeed. For, make no mistake: if you are really going to try to meet all the demands made on the natural self, it will not have enough left over to live on. The more you obey your conscience, the more your conscience will demand of you. And your natural self, which is thus being starved and hampered and worried at every turn, will get angrier and angrier. In the end, you will either give up trying to be good, or else become one of those people who, as they say, "live for others" but always in a discontented, grumbling way—always wondering why the others do not notice it more and always making a martyr of yourself. And once you have become that, you will be a far greater pest to anyone who has to live with you than you would have been if you had remained frankly selfish.

The Christian way is different: harder, and easier. Christ says "Give me All. I don't want so much of your time and so much of your money and so much of your work: I want You. I have not come to torment your natural self, but to kill it. No half-measures are any good. I don't want to cut off a branch here and a branch there, I want to have the whole tree down. I don't want to drill the tooth, or crown it, or stop it, but to have it out. Hand over the whole natural self, all the desires which you think innocent as well as the ones you think wicked—the whole outfit. I will give you a new self instead. In fact, I will give you Myself: my own will shall become yours."

Both harder and easier than what we are all trying to do. You have noticed, I expect, that Christ Himself sometimes describes the Christian way as very hard, sometimes as very easy. He says, "Take up your Cross"—in other words, it is like going to be beaten to death in a concentration camp. Next minute he says, "My yoke is easy and my burden light." He means both. And one can just see why both are true.

Teachers will tell you that the laziest boy in the class is the one who works hardest in the end. They mean this. If you give two boys, say, a proposition in geometry to do, the one who is prepared to take trouble will try to understand it. The lazy boy will try to learn it by heart because, for the moment, that needs less effort. But six months later, when they are preparing for an exam, that lazy boy is doing hours and hours of miserable drudgery over things the other boy understands, and positively enjoys, in a few minutes. Laziness means more work in the long run. Or look at it this way. In a battle, or in mountain climbing, there is often one thing which it takes a lot of pluck to do; but it is also, in the long run, the safest thing to do. If you funk it, you will find yourself, hours later, in far worse danger. The cowardly thing is also the most dangerous thing.

It is like that here. The terrible thing, the almost impossible thing, is to hand over your whole self—all your wishes and precautions—to Christ. But it is far easier than what we are all trying to do instead. For what we are trying to do is to remain what we call "ourselves," to keep personal happiness as our great aim in life, and yet at the same time be "good." We are all trying to let our mind and heart go their own way—centered on money or pleasure or ambition—and hoping, in spite of this, to behave honestly and chastely and humbly. And that is exactly what Christ warned us you could not do. As He said, a thistle cannot produce figs. If I am a field that contains nothing but grass-seed, I cannot produce wheat. Cutting the grass may keep it short: but I shall still produce grass and no wheat. If I want to produce wheat, the change must go deeper than the surface. I must be ploughed up and resown.

That is why the real problem of the Christian life comes where people do not usually look for it. It comes the very moment you wake up each morning. All your wishes and hopes for the day rush at you like wild animals. And the first job each morning consists simply in shoving them all back; in listening to that other voice, taking that other point of view, letting that other larger, stronger, quieter life come flowing in. And so on, all day. Standing back from all your natural fussings and frettings; coming in out of the wind.

We can only do it for moments at first. But from those moments the new sort of life will be spreading through our system: because now we are letting Him work at the right part of us. It is the difference between paint, which is merely laid on the surface, and a dye or stain which soaks right through. He never talked vague, idealistic gas. When He said, "Be perfect," He meant it. He meant that we must go in for the full treatment. It is hard; but the sort of compromise we are all hankering after is harder—in fact, it is impossible. It may be hard for an egg to turn into a bird: it would be a jolly sight harder for it to learn to fly while remaining an egg. We are like eggs at present. And you cannot go on indefinitely being just an ordinary, decent egg. We must be hatched or go bad.

May I come back to what I said before? This is the whole of Christianity. There is nothing else. It is so easy to get muddled about that. It is easy to think that the Church has a lot of different objects—education, building, missions, holding services. Just as it is easy to think the State has a lot of different objects—military, political, economic, and what not. But in a way things are much simpler than that. The State exists simply to promote and to protect the ordinary happiness of human beings in this life. A husband and wife chatting over a fire, a couple of friends having a game of darts in a pub, a man reading a book in his own room or digging in his own garden—that is what the State is there for. And unless they are helping to increase and prolong and protect such moments, all the laws, parliaments, armies, courts, police, economics, etc., are simply a waste of time. In the same way the Church exists for nothing else but to draw men into Christ, to make them little Christs. If they are not doing that, all the cathedrals, clergy, missions, sermons, even the Bible itself, are simply a waste of time. God became Man for no other purpose. It is even doubtful, you know, whether the whole universe was created for any other purpose. It says in the Bible that the whole universe was made for Christ and that everything is to be gathered together in Him. I do not suppose any of us can understand how this will happen as regards the whole universe. We do not know what (if anything) lives in the parts of it that are millions of miles away from this Earth. Even on this Earth we do not know how it applies to things other than men. After all, that is what you would expect. We have been shown the plan only insofar as it concerns ourselves.

I sometimes like to imagine that I can just see how it might apply to other things. I think I can see how the higher animals are in a sense drawn into Man when he loves them and makes them (as he does) much more nearly human than they would otherwise be. I can even see a sense in which the dead things and plants are drawn into Man as he studies them and uses and appreciates them. And if there were intelligent creatures in other worlds they might do the same with their worlds. It might be that when intelligent creatures entered into Christ they would, in that way, bring all the other things in along with them. But I do not know: it is only a guess.

What we have been told is how we men can be drawn into Christ—can become part of that wonderful present

which the young Prince of the universe wants to offer to
His Father—that present which is Himself and therefore us
in Him. It is the only thing we were made for. And there
are strange, exciting hints in the Bible that when we are
drawn in, a great many other things in Nature will begin to
come right. The bad dream will be over: it will be morning.

Apologetics

APOLOGETICS MEANS, of course, Defense. The first question
is—what do you propose to defend? Christianity, of
course. . . .

We are to defend Christianity itself—the faith preached
by the Apostles, attested by the Martyrs, embodied in the
Creeds, expounded by the Fathers. . . .

The great difficulty is to get modern audiences to realize
that you are preaching Christianity solely and simply because you happen to think it *true;* they always suppose you
are preaching it because you like it or think it good for society or something of that sort. . . .

Secondly, this scrupulous care to preserve the Christian
message as something distinct from one's own ideas, has
one very good effect upon the apologist himself. It forces
him, again and again, to face up to those elements in original Christianity which he personally finds obscure or repul-
sive. He is saved from the temptation to skip, or slur, or ignore what he finds disagreeable. . . .

From this there follows a corollary about the Apologist's
private reading. There are two questions he will naturally
ask himself. (1) Have I been "keeping up," keeping abreast
of recent movements in theology? (2) Have I stood firm . . .

amidst all these "winds of doctrine" (Ephesians 4:14)? I want to say emphatically that the second question is far the more important of the two. . . .

I am speaking, so far, of theological reading. Scientific reading is a different matter. . . .

While we are on the subject of science, let me digress for a moment. I believe that any Christian who is qualified to write a good popular book on any science may do much more by that than by any directly apologetic work. . . .

Our business is to present that which is timeless (the same yesterday, today, and tomorrow) in the particular language of our own age. . . .

This raises the question of Theology and Politics. The nearest I can get to a settlement of the frontier problem between them is this:—that Theology teaches us what ends are desirable and what means are lawful, while Politics teaches what means are effective. . . .

Our great danger at present is lest the Church should continue to practice a merely missionary technique in what has become a missionary situation. . . .

(1) I find that the uneducated Englishman is an almost total skeptic about History. . . .

(2) He has a distrust (very rational in the state of his knowledge) of ancient texts. . . .

(3) A sense of sin is almost totally lacking. . . .

(4) We must learn the language of our audience. . . . You must translate every bit of your Theology into the Vernacular. . . .

Do not attempt to water Christianity down. . . .

One last word. I have found that nothing is more dangerous to one's own faith than the work of an apologist. No doctrine of that Faith seems to me so spectral, so unreal as one that I have just successfully defended in a public debate. For a moment, you see, it has seemed to rest on oneself: as a result, when you go away from that debate, it seems no stronger than that weak pillar. That is why we apologists take our lives in our hands and can be saved only by falling back continually from the web of our own arguments, as from our intellectual counters, into the Reality— from Christian apologetics into Christ Himself.

Money

THERE IS ONE BIT of advice given to us by the ancient heathen Greeks, and by the Jews in the Old Testament, and by the great Christian teachers of the Middle Ages, which the modern economic system has completely disobeyed. All these people told us not to lend money at interest: and lending money at interest—what we call investment—is the basis of our whole system. Now it may not absolutely follow that we are wrong. Some people say that when Moses and Aristotle and the Christians agreed in forbidding interest (or "usury" as they called it), they could not foresee the joint stock company, and were only thinking of the private moneylender, and that, therefore, we need not bother about what they said. That is a question I cannot decide on. I am not an economist and I simply do not know whether the investment system is responsible for the state we are in or not. This is where we want the Christian economist. But I should not have been honest if I had not told you that three great civilizations had agreed (or so it seems at first sight) in condemning the very thing on which we have based our whole life.

Gift-love and Need-love

"GOD IS LOVE," says St. John. When I first tried to write
[*The Four Loves*], I thought that his maxim would provide
me with a very plain highroad through the whole subject. I
thought I should be able to say that human loves deserved
to be called loves at all just insofar as they resembled that
Love which is God. The first distinction I made was therefore between what I called Gift-love and Need-love. The
typical example of Gift-love would be that love which
moves a man to work, and plan, and save for the future
well-being of his family which he will die without sharing
or seeing; of the second, that which sends a lonely or fright-
ened child to its mother's arms.

There was no doubt which was more like Love Himself.
Divine Love is Gift-love. The Father gives all He is and has
to the Son. The Son gives Himself back to the Father, and
gives Himself to the world, and for the world to the Father,
and thus gives the world (in Himself) back to the Father
too.

And what, on the other hand, can be less like anything
we believe of God's life than Need-love? He lacks nothing,
but our Need-love, as Plato saw, is "the son of Poverty." It
is the accurate reflection in consciousness of our actual nature. We are born helpless. As soon as we are fully conscious, we discover loneliness. We need others physically,
emotionally, intellectually; we need them if we are to know
anything, even ourselves.

Appreciative Love

NEED-LOVE CRIES TO GOD from our poverty; Gift-love longs
to serve, or even to suffer for, God; Appreciative love says:
"We give thanks to Thee for Thy great glory." Need-love
says of a woman "I cannot live without her"; Gift-love
longs to give her happiness, comfort, protection—if possible, wealth; Appreciative love gazes and holds its breath
and is silent, rejoices that such a wonder should exist even
if not for him, will not be wholly dejected by losing her,
would rather have it so than never to have seen her at all.

We murder to dissect. In actual life, thank God, the three
elements of love mix and succeed one another, moment by
moment. Perhaps none of them except Need-love ever
exists alone, in "chemical" purity, for more than a few sec-
onds. And perhaps that is because nothing about us except
our neediness is, in this life, permanent.

Love of Nature

FOR SOME PEOPLE, perhaps especially for Englishmen and
Russians, what we call "the love of nature" is a permanent
and serious sentiment. I mean here that love of nature
which cannot be adequately classified simply as an instance
of our love for beauty. Of course, many natural objects—
trees, flowers, and animals—are beautiful. But the nature
lovers whom I have in mind are not very much concerned

with individual beautiful objects of that sort. The man who
is distracts them. An enthusiastic botanist is for them a
dreadful companion on a ramble. He is always stopping to
draw their attention to particulars. Nor are they looking for
"views" or landscapes. Wordsworth, their spokesman,
strongly deprecates this. It leads to "a comparison of scene
with scene," makes you "pamper" yourself with "meager
novelties of color and proportion." While you are busying
yourself with this critical and discriminating activity, you
lose what really matters—the "moods of time and season,"
the "spirit" of the place. And, of course, Wordsworth is
right. That is why, if you love nature in his fashion, a landscape painter is (out of doors) an even worse companion
than a botanist.

It is the "moods" or the "spirit" that matter. Nature
lovers want to receive as fully as possible whatever nature,
at each particular time and place, is, so to speak, saying.
The obvious richness, grace, and harmony of some scenes
are no more precious to them than the grimness, bleakness,
terror, monotony, or "visionary dreariness" of others. The
featureless itself gets from them a willing response. It is one
more word uttered by nature. They lay themselves bare to
the sheer quality of every countryside, every hour of the
day. They want to absorb it into themselves, to be colored
through and through by it.

Love of Country

IN REALITY it contains many ingredients, of which many
different blends are possible.

First, there is love of home, of the place we grew up in or
the places, perhaps many, which have been our homes;

and of all the places fairly near these and fairly like them; love of old acquaintances, of familiar sights, sounds, and smells. . . .

The second ingredient is a particular attitude to our country's past. I mean to that past as it lives in popular imagination; the great deeds of our ancestors. . . .

The third thing is not a sentiment but a belief: a firm, even prosaic belief that our own nation, in sober fact, has long been, and still is markedly superior to all others. . . . I once ventured to say to an old clergyman who was voicing this sort of patriotism, "But, sir, aren't we told that *every* people thinks its own men the bravest and its own women the fairest in the world?" He replied with total gravity—he could not have been graver if he had been saying the Creed at the altar—"Yes, but in England it's true." To be sure, this conviction had not made my friend (God rest his soul) a villain; only an extremely lovable old ass. It can however produce asses that kick and bite. On the lunatic fringe it may shade off into that popular Racialism which Christianity and science equally forbid.

Storge or Affection

AFFECTION . . . is the humblest love. It gives itself no airs. People can be proud of being "in love," or of friendship. Affection is modest—even furtive and shamefaced. Often when I had remarked on the affection quite often found between cat and dog, my friend replied, "yes. But I bet no dog would ever confess it to the other dogs." That is at least a good caricature of much human Affection. "Let homely faces stay at home," says Comus. Now Affection has a very homely face. So have many of those for whom we feel it. It is no proof of our refinement or perceptiveness that we love them; nor that they love us. What I have called Appreciative love is no basic element in Affection. It usually needs absence or bereavement to set us praising those to whom only Affection binds us. We take them for granted: and this taking for granted, which is an outrage in erotic love, is here right and proper up to a point. It fits the comfortable, quiet nature of the feeling. Affection would not be affection if it was loudly and frequently expressed; to produce it in public is like getting your household furniture out for a move. It did very well in its place, but it looks shabby or tawdry or grotesque in the sunshine. Affection almost slinks or seeps through our lives. It lives with humble, undress, private things; soft slippers, old clothes, old jokes, the thump of a sleepy dog's tail on the kitchen floor, the sound of a sewing machine, a gollywog left on the lawn.

But I must at once correct myself. I am talking of Affection as it is when it exists apart from the other loves. It often does so exist; often not. As gin is not only a drink in itself but also a base for many mixed drinks, so Affection, besides being a love itself, can enter into the other loves and color them all through and become the very medium in which from day to day they operate. They would not perhaps wear very well without it. To make a friend is not the same as to become affectionate. But when your friend has become an old friend, all those things about him which had originally nothing to do with the friendship become familiar and dear with familiarity. As for erotic love, I can imagine nothing more disagreeable than to experience it for more than a very short time without this homespun clothing of affection. That would be a most uneasy condition, either too angelic, or too animal, or each by turn; never quite great enough or little enough for man. There is indeed a peculiar charm, both in Friendship and in Eros, about those moments when Appreciative love lies, as it were, curled up asleep, and the mere ease and ordinariness of the relationship (free as solitude, yet neither is alone) wraps us round. No need to talk. No need to make love. No needs at all except perhaps to stir the fire.

Philia or Friendship

[COMPANIONSHIP] IS OFTEN CALLED Friendship, and many people, when they speak of their "friends" mean only their companions. But it is not Friendship in the sense I give to the word. . . .

Friendship arises out of mere Companionship when two or more of the companions discover that they have in common some insight which the others do not share and which, till that moment, each believed to be his own unique treasure (or burden). The typical expression of opening Friendship would be something like, "What? You too? I thought I was the only one." We can imagine that among those early hunters and warriors single individuals—one in a century? one in a thousand years?—saw what others did not; saw that the deer was beautiful as well as edible, that hunting was fun as well as necessary, dreamed that his gods might be not only powerful but holy. But as long as each of these percipient persons dies without finding a kindred soul, nothing (I suspect) will come of it; art, or sport, or spiritual religion will not be born. It is when two such persons discover one another, when, whether with immense difficulties and semiarticulate fumblings or with what would seem to us amazing and elliptical speed, they share their vision—it is then that Friendship is born. And instantly they stand together in an immense solitude.

Lovers seek privacy. Friends find this solitude about them, this barrier between them and the herd, whether they want it or not. They would be glad to reduce it. The first two would be glad to find a third.

In our own time Friendship arises in the same way. For us, of course, the shared activity and therefore the companionship on which Friendship supervenes will not often be a bodily one like hunting or fighting. It may be a common religion, common studies, a common profession, even a common recreation. All who share it will be our companions; but one or two or three who share something more will be our Friends. In this kind of love, as Emerson said, *Do you love me?* means *Do you see the same truth?*—Or at least, "Do you *care about* the same truth?" The man who agrees with us that some question, little regarded by others, is of great importance can be our Friend. He need not agree with us about the answer.

Notice that Friendship thus repeats on a more individual and less socially necessary level the character of the Companionship which was its matrix. The Companionship was between people who were doing something together—hunting, studying, painting, or what you will. The Friends will still be doing something together, but something more inward, less widely shared, and less easily defined; still hunters, but of some immaterial quarry; still collaborating, but in some work the world does not, or not yet, take account of; still traveling companions, but on a different kind of journey. Hence we picture lovers face to face but Friends side by side; their eyes look ahead.

Eros and Venus

BY EROS I mean . . . that state which we call "being in love"; or, if you prefer, that kind of love which lovers are "in". . . . The carnal or animally sexual element within Eros, I intend (following an old usage) to call Venus. . . .

To the evolutionist Eros (the human variation) will be something that grows out of Venus, a late complication and development of the immemorial biological impulse. We must not assume, however, that this is necessarily what happens within the consciousness of the individual. There may be those who have first felt mere sexual appetite for a woman and then gone on to a later stage to "fall in love with her." But I doubt if this is at all common. Very often what comes first is simply a delighted preoccupation with the Beloved—a general, unspecified preoccupation with her in her totality. A man in this state really hasn't leisure to think of sex. He is too busy thinking of a person. The fact that she is a woman is far less important than the fact that she is herself. He is full of desire, but the desire may not be sexually toned. If you ask him what he wanted, the true reply would often be, "To go on thinking of her." He is love's contemplative. And when at a later stage the explicitly sexual element awakes, he will not feel (unless scientific theories are influencing him) that this had all along been the root of the whole matter. He is more likely to feel that the incoming tide of Eros, having demolished many sand castles and made islands of many rocks, has now at last with a triumphant seventh wave flooded this part of his nature also—the little pool of ordinary sexuality which was there on his beach before the tide came in. Eros enters him like an invader, taking over and reorganizing, one by one, the institutions of a conquered country. It may have taken over many others before it reaches the sex in him; and it will reorganize that too. . . .

We must not be totally serious about Venus. Indeed we can't be totally serious without doing violence to our humanity. It is not for nothing that every language and literature in the world is full of jokes about sex. Many of them may be dull or disgusting and nearly all of them are old. But we must insist that they embody an attitude to Venus which in the long run endangers the Christian life far less than a reverential gravity. We must not attempt to find an absolute in the flesh. Banish play and laughter from the bed of love and you may let in a false goddess. She will be even falser than the Aphrodite of the Greeks; for they, even while they worshiped her, knew that she was "laughter-loving." The mass of the people are perfectly right in their conviction that Venus is a partly comic spirit. We are under no obligation at all to sing all our love duets in the throbbing, world-without-end, heartbreaking manner of Tristan and Isolde; let us often sing like Papageno and Papagena instead. . . .

I can hardly help regarding it as one of God's jokes that a passion so soaring, so apparently transcendent, as Eros, should thus be linked in incongruous symbiosis with a bodily appetite which, like any other appetite, tactlessly reveals its connections with such mundane factors as weather, health, diet, circulation, and digestion. In Eros at times we seem to be flying; Venus gives us the sudden twitch that reminds us we are really captive balloons. It is a continual demonstration of the truth that we are composite creatures, rational animals, akin on one side to the angels, on the other to tomcats. It is a bad thing not to be able to take a joke. Worse, not to take a divine joke; made, I grant you, at our expense, but also (who doubts it?) for our endless benefit.

Agape or Charity

WE MUST NOT begin with mysticism, with the creature's love for God, or with the wonderful foretastes of the fruition of God vouchsafed to some in their earthly life. We begin at the real beginning, with love as the Divine energy. This primal love is Gift-love. In God there is no hunger that needs to be filled, only plenteousness that desires to give. The doctrine that God was under no necessity to create is not a piece of dry scholastic speculation. It is essential. Without it we can hardly avoid the conception of what I can only call a "managerial" God; a Being whose function or nature is to "run" the universe, who stands to it as a headmaster to a school or a hotelier to a hotel. But to be sovereign of the universe is no great matter to God. In Himself, at home in "the land of the Trinity," he is Sovereign of a far greater realm. We must keep always before our eyes that vision of Lady Julian's in which God carried in His hand a little object like a nut, and that nut was "all that is made." God, who needs nothing, loves into existence wholly superfluous creatures in order that He may love and perfect them. He creates the universe, already foreseeing—or should we say "seeing"? there are no tenses in God—the buzzing cloud of flies about the cross, the flayed back pressed against the uneven stake, the nails driven through the mesial nerves, the repeated incipient suffocation as the body droops, the repeated torture of back and arms as it is time after time, for breath's sake, hitched up. If I may dare the biological image, God is a "host" who deliberately creates His own parasites; causes us to be that we may exploit and "take advantage of" Him. Herein is love. This is the diagram of Love Himself, the inventor of all loves.

God, as Creator of nature, implants in us both Gift-loves and Need-loves. The Gift-loves are natural images of Himself; proximities to Him by resemblance which are not necessarily and in all men proximities of approach. A devoted mother, a beneficent ruler or teacher, may give and give, continually exhibiting the likeness, without making the approach. The Need-loves, so far as I have been able to see, have no resemblance to the Love which God is. They are rather correlatives, opposites; not as evil is the opposite of good, of course, but as the form of the blancmange is an opposite to the form of the mold.

But in addition to these natural loves God can bestow a far better gift; or rather, since our minds must divide and pigeonhole, two gifts.

He communicates to men a share of His own Gift-love. This is different from the Gift-loves He has built into their nature. These never quite seek simply the good of the loved object for the object's own sake. They are biased in favor of those goods they can themselves bestow, or those which they would like best themselves, or those which fit in with a preconceived picture of the life they want the object to lead. But Divine Gift-love—Love Himself working in a man—is wholly disinterested and desires what is simply best for the beloved. Again, natural Gift-love is always directed to objects which the lover finds in some way intrinsically lovable—objects to which Affection, or Eros, or a shared point of view attracts him, or, failing that, to the grateful and the deserving, or perhaps to those whose helplessness is of a winning and appealing kind. But Divine Gift-love in the man enables him to love what is not naturally lovable; lepers, criminals, enemies, morons, the sulky, the superior, and the sneering. Finally, by a high paradox, God enables men to have a Gift-love toward Himself. There is, of course, a sense in which no one can give to God anything which is not already His; and if it is already His, what have you given? But since it is only too obvious that we can withhold ourselves, our wills and hearts, from God, we can, in that sense, also give them. What is His by right and would not exist for a moment if it ceased to be His (as the song is the singer's), He has nevertheless made ours in such a way that we can freely offer it back to Him. "Our wills are ours to make them Thine." And as all Christians know, there is another way of giving to God; every stranger whom we feed or clothe is Christ. And this apparently is Gift-love to God whether we know it or not. Love Himself can work in those who know nothing of Him. The "sheep" in the parable had no idea either of the God hidden in the prisoner whom they visited or of the God hidden in themselves when they made the visit. (I take the whole parable to be about the judgment of the heathen. For it begins by saying, in the Greek, that the Lord will summon all "the nations" before Him—presumably, the Gentiles, the *Goyim*.)

That such a Gift-love comes by Grace and should be called Charity, everyone will agree.

"Love Thy Neighbor"

IT IS A serious thing to live in a society of possible gods and goddesses, to remember that the dullest and most uninteresting person you talk to may one day be a creature which, if you saw it now, you would be strongly tempted to worship, or else a horror and a corruption such as you now meet, if at all, only in a nightmare. All day long we are, in some degree, helping each other to one or other of these destinations. It is in the light of these overwhelming possibilities, it is with the awe and the circumspection proper to them, that we should conduct all our dealings with one another, all friendships, all loves, all play, all politics. There are no ordinary people. You have never talked to a mere mortal. Nations, cultures, arts, civilization—these are mortal, and their life is to ours as the life of a gnat. But it is immortals whom we joke with, work with, marry, snub, and exploit—immortal horrors or everlasting splendors. This does not mean that we are to be perpetually solemn. We must play. But our merriment must be of that kind (and it is, in fact, the merriest kind) which exists between people who have, from the outset, taken each other seriously—no flippancy, no superiority, no presumption. And our charity must be a real and costly love, with deep feeling for the sins in spite of which we love the sinner—no mere tolerance or indulgence which parodies love as flippancy parodies merriment. Next to the Blessed Sacrament itself, your neighbor is the holiest object presented to your senses. If he is your Christian neighbor, he is holy in almost the same way, for in him also Christ *vere latitat*—the glorifier and the glorified, Glory Himself, is truly hidden.

Sex

SEX IN ITSELF cannot be moral or immoral any more than gravitation or nutrition. The sexual behavior of human beings can. And like their economic, or political, or agricultural, or parental, or filial behavior, it is sometimes good and sometimes bad. And the sexual act, when lawful—which means chiefly when consistent with good faith and charity—can, like all other merely natural acts ("whether we eat or drink, etc.," as the Apostle says), be done to the glory of God, and will then be holy. And like other natural acts it is sometimes so done, and sometimes not.

Marriage

THE CHRISTIAN IDEA of marriage is based on Christ's words that a man and wife are to be regarded as a single organism—for that is what the words "one flesh" would be in modern English. And the Christians believe that when He said this He was not expressing a sentiment but stating a fact—just as one is stating a fact when one says that a lock and its key are one mechanism, or that a violin and a bow are one musical instrument. The inventor of the human machine was telling us that its two halves, the male and the female, were made to be combined together in pairs, not simply on the sexual level, but totally combined. The monstrosity of sexual intercourse outside marriage is that those who indulge in it are trying to isolate one kind of union (the sexual) from all the other kinds of union which were intended to go along with it and make up the total union. The Christian attitude does not mean that there is anything wrong about sexual pleasure, any more than about the pleasure of eating. It means that you must not isolate that pleasure and try to get it by itself, any more than you ought to try to get the pleasures of taste without swallowing and digesting, by chewing things and spitting them out again.

✶

One thing . . . marriage has done for me. I can never again believe that religion is manufactured out of our unconscious, starved desires and is a substitute for sex. For those few years H. [his wife Helen Joy] and I feasted on love; every mode of it—solemn and merry, romantic and realistic, sometimes as dramatic as a thunderstorm, sometimes as comfortable and unemphatic as putting on your soft slippers. No cranny of heart or body remained unsatisfied. If God were a substitute for love, we ought to have lost all interest in Him. Who'd bother about substitutes when he has the thing itself? But that isn't what happens. We both knew we wanted something besides one another—quite a different kind of something, a quite different kind of want. You might as well say that when lovers have one another, they will never want to read, or eat—or breathe. . . .

The most precious gift that marriage gave me was this constant impact of something very close and intimate yet all the time unmistakably other, resistant—in a word, real.

Divorce

CHRISTIANITY TEACHES that marriage is for life. There is, of course, a difference between Churches: some do not admit divorce at all; some allow it reluctantly in very special cases. It is a great pity that Christians should disagree about such a question; but for an ordinary layman the thing to notice is that Churches all agree with one another about marriage a great deal more than any of them agrees with the outside world. I mean, they all regard divorce as something like cutting up a living body, as a kind of surgical operation. Some of them think the operation so violent that it cannot be done at all; others admit it as a desperate remedy in extreme cases. They are all agreed that it is more like having both your legs cut off than it is like dissolving a business partnership or even deserting a regiment. What they all disagree with is the modern view that it is a simple readjustment of partners, to be made whenever people feel they are no longer in love with one another, or when either of them falls in love with someone else.

Intercourse in the Afterlife

THE LETTER AND SPIRIT of Scripture, and of all Christianity, forbid us to suppose that life in the New Creation will be a sexual life; and this reduces our imagination to the withering alternative either of bodies which are hardly recognizable as human bodies at all or else of a perpetual fast. As regards the fast, I think our present outlook might be like that of a small boy who, on being told that the sexual act was the highest bodily pleasure, should immediately ask whether you ate chocolates at the same time. On receiving the answer "No," he might regard absence of chocolates as the chief characteristic of sexuality. In vain would you tell him that the reason why lovers in their carnal raptures don't bother about chocolates is that they have something better to think of. The boy knows chocolate: he does not know the positive thing that excludes it. We are in the same position. We know the sexual life; we do not know, except in glimpses, the other thing which, in Heaven, will leave no room for it. Hence where fullness awaits us we anticipate fasting. In denying that sexual life, as we now understand it, makes any part of the final beatitude, it is not, of course, necessary to suppose that the distinction of sexes will disappear. What is no longer needed for biological purposes may be expected to survive for splendor. Sexuality is the instrument both of virginity and conjugal virtue; neither men nor women will be asked to throw away weapons they have used victoriously. It is the beaten and the fugitives who throw away their swords. The conquerors sheathe theirs and retain them. . . .

I am well aware that this last . . . may seem to many

readers unfortunate and to some comic. But that very comedy, as I must repeatedly insist, is the symptom of our estrangement, as spirits, from Nature and our estrangement, as animals, from Spirit. The whole conception of the New Creation involves the belief that this estrangement will be healed. A curious consequence will follow. The archaic type of thought which could not clearly distinguish spiritual "Heaven" from the sky, is from our point of view a confused type of thought. But it also resembles and anticipates a type of thought which will one day be true. That archaic sort of thinking will become simply the correct sort when Nature and Spirit are fully harmonized—when Spirit rides Nature so perfectly that the two together make rather a *Centaur* than a mounted knight. I do not mean necessarily that the blending of Heaven and sky, in particular, will turn out to be specially true, but that that kind of blending will accurately mirror the reality which will then exist. There will be no room to get the finest razor blade of thought in between Spirit and Nature. Every state of affairs in the New Nature will be the perfect expression of a spiritual state and every spiritual state the perfect informing of, and bloom upon, a state of affairs; one with it as the perfume with a flower or the "spirit" of great poetry with its form. There is thus in the history of human thought, as elsewhere, a pattern of death and rebirth. The old, richly imaginative thought which still survives in Plato has to submit to the deathlike, but indispensable, process of logical analysis: nature and spirit, matter and mind, fact and myth, the literal and the metaphorical, have to be more and more sharply separated, till at last a purely mathematical universe and a purely subjective mind confront one another across an unbridgeable chasm. But from this descent also, if thought itself is to survive, there must be reascent and the Christian conception provides for it. Those who attain the glorious resurrection will see the dry bones clothed again with flesh, and the fact and the myth remarried, the literal and the metaphorical rushing together.

Christmas and Xmas

CHRISTMAS CARDS in general and the whole vast commercial drive called "Xmas" are one of my pet abominations; I wish they could die away and leave the Christian feast unentangled. Not of course that even secular festivities are, on their own level, an evil; but the labored and organized jollity of this—the spurious childlikeness—the half-hearted and sometimes rather profane attempts to keep up some superficial connection with the Nativity—are disgusting.

✳

Three things go by the name of Christmas. One is a religious festival. This is important and obligatory for Christians; but as it can be of no interest to anyone else, I shall naturally say no more about it here. The second (it has complex historical connections with the first, but we needn't go into them) is a popular holiday, an occasion for merrymaking and hospitality. If it were my business to have a "view" on this, I should say that I much approve of merrymaking. But what I approve of much more is everybody minding his own business. I see no reason why I should volunteer views as to how other people should spend their own money in their own leisure among their own friends. It is highly probable that they want my advice on such matters as little as I want theirs. But the third thing called Christmas is unfortunately everyone's business.

I mean of course the commercial racket. The interchange

of presents was a very small ingredient in the older English festivity. Mr. Pickwick took a cod with him to Dingley Dell; the reformed Scrooge ordered a turkey for his clerk; lovers sent love gifts; toys and fruit were given to children. But the idea that not only all friends but even all acquaintances should give one another presents, or at least send one another cards, is quite modern and has been forced upon us by the shopkeepers. Neither of these circumstances is in itself a reason for condemning it. I condemn it on the following grounds.

1. It gives on the whole much more pain than pleasure. You have only to stay over Christmas with a family who seriously try to "keep" it (in its third, or commercial, aspect) in order to see that the thing is a nightmare. Long before December 25th everyone is worn out—physically worn out by weeks of daily struggle in overcrowded shops, mentally worn out by the effort to remember all the right recipients and to think out suitable gifts for them. They are in no trim for merrymaking; much less (if they should want to) to take part in a religious act. They look far more as if there had been a long illness in the house.

2. Most of it is involuntary. The modern rule is that anyone can force you to give him a present by sending you a quite unprovoked present of his own. It is almost a blackmail. Who has not heard the wail of despair, and indeed of resentment, when, at the last moment, just as everyone hoped that the nuisance was over for one more year, the unwanted gift from Mrs. Busy (whom we hardly remember) flops unwelcomed through the letter-box, and back to the dreadful shops one of us has to go?

3. Things are given as presents which no mortal ever bought for himself—gaudy and useless gadgets, "novelties" because no one was ever fool enough to make their like before. Have we really no better use for materials and for human skill and time than to spend them on all this rubbish?

4. The nuisance. For after all, during the racket we still have all our ordinary and necessary shopping to do, and the racket trebles the labor of it.

We are told that the whole dreary business must go on because it is good for trade. It is in fact merely one annual symptom of that lunatic condition of our country, and indeed of the world, in which everyone lives by persuading everyone else to buy things. I don't know the way out. But can it really be my duty to buy and receive masses of junk every winter just to help the shopkeepers? If the worst comes to the worst I'd sooner give them money for nothing and write it off as a charity. For nothing? Why, better for nothing than for a nuisance.

The Ego and the Self

THE SELF CAN BE regarded in two ways. On the one hand, it is God's creature, an occasion of love and rejoicing; now, indeed, hateful in condition, but to be pitied and healed. On the other hand, it is that one self of all others which is called *I* and *me*, and which on that ground puts forward an irrational claim to preference. This claim is to be not only hated, but simply killed; "never," as George Macdonald says, "to be allowed a moment's respite from eternal death." The Christian must wage endless war against the *ego* as *ego*: but he loves and approves selves as such, though not their sins. The very self-love which he has to reject is to him a specimen of how he ought to feel to all selves; and he may hope that when he has truly learned (which will hardly be in this life) to love his neighbor as himself, he may then be able to love himself as his neighbor: that is, with charity instead of partiality.

The other kind of self-hatred, on the contrary, hates selves as such. It begins by accepting the special value of the particular self called *me;* then, wounded in its pride to find that such a darling object should be so disappointing, it seeks revenge, first upon that self, then on all. Deeply egoistic, but now with an inverted egoism, it uses the revealing argument, "I don't spare myself"—and becomes like the centurion in Tacitus, "more relentless because he had endured it himself."

The wrong asceticism torments the self: the right kind kills the selfness. We must die daily: but it is better to love the self than to love nothing, and to pity the self than to pity no one.

The Airplane, the Wireless, and the Contraceptive

"MAN'S CONQUEST of Nature" is an expression often used to describe the progress of applied science. "Man has Nature whacked" said someone to a friend of mine not long ago. In their context the words had a certain tragic beauty, for the speaker was dying of tuberculosis. "No matter," he said, "I know I'm one of the casualties. Of course there are casualties on the winning as well as on the losing side. But that doesn't alter the fact that it is winning." I have chosen this story as my point of departure in order to make it clear that I do not wish to disparage all that is really beneficial in the process described as "Man's conquest," much less all the real devotion and self-sacrifice that [have] gone to make it possible. But having done so I must proceed to analyze this conception a little more closely. In what sense is Man the possessor of increasing power over Nature?

Let us consider three typical examples: the airplane, the wireless, and the contraceptive. In a civilized community, in peacetime, anyone who can pay for them may use these things. But it cannot strictly be said that when he does so he is exercising his own proper or individual power over Nature. If I pay you to carry me, I am not therefore myself a strong man. Any or all of the three things I have mentioned can be withheld from some men by other men—by those who sell, or those who allow the sale, or those who own the sources of production, or those who make the goods. What we call Man's power is, in reality, a power possessed by some men which they may, or may not, allow other men to profit by. Again, as regards the powers manifested in the airplane or the wireless, Man is as much the patient or subject as the possessor, since he is the target both for bombs and for propaganda. And as regards contraceptives, there is a paradoxical, negative sense in which all possible future generations are the patients or subjects of a power wielded by those already alive. By contraception simply, they are denied existence; by contraception used as a means of selective breeding, they are, without their concurring voice, made to be what one generation, for its own reasons, may choose to prefer. From this point of view, what we call Man's power over Nature turns out to be a power exercised by some men over other men with Nature as its instrument.

It is, of course, a commonplace to complain that men have hitherto used badly, and against their fellows, the powers that science has given them. But that is not the point I am trying to make. I am not speaking of particular corruptions and abuses which an increase of moral virtue would cure: I am considering what the thing called "Man's power over Nature" must always and essentially be. No doubt, the picture could be modified by public ownership of raw materials and factories and public control of scientific research. But unless we have a world state this will still mean the power of one nation over others. And even within the world state or the nation it will mean (in principle) the power of majorities over minorities, and (in the concrete) of a government over the people. And all long-term exercises of power, especially in breeding, must mean the power of earlier generations over later ones.

The latter point is not always sufficiently emphasized, because those who write on social matters have not yet learned to imitate the physicists by always including Time among the dimensions. In order to understand fully what Man's power over Nature, and therefore the power of some men over other men, really means, we must picture the race extended in time from the date of its emergence to that of its extinction. Each generation exercises power over its successors: and each, insofar as it modifies the environment bequeathed to it and rebels against tradition, resists and limits the power of its predecessors. This modifies the picture which is sometimes painted of a progressive emancipation from tradition and a progressive control of natural processes resulting in a continual increase of human power. In reality, of course, if any one age really attains, by eugenics and scientific education, the power to make its descendants what it pleases, all men who live after it are the patients of that power. They are weaker, not stronger: for though we may have put wonderful machines in their hands we have preordained how they are to use them. And if, as is almost certain, the age which had thus attained maximum power over posterity were also the age most emancipated from tradition, it would be engaged in reducing the power of its predecessors almost as drastically as that of its successors. And we must also remember that, quite apart from this, the later a generation comes—the nearer it lives to that date at which the species become extinct—the less power it will have in the forward direction, because its subjects will be so few. There is therefore no question of a power vested in the race as a whole steadily growing as long as the race survives. The last men, far from being the heirs of power, will be of all men most subject to the dead hand of the great planners and conditioners and will themselves exercise least power upon the future. The real picture is that of one dominant age—let us suppose the hundredth century A.D.—which resists all previous ages most sucessfully and dominates all subsequent ages most irresistibly, and thus is the real master of the human species. But even within this master generation (itself an infinitesimal minority of the species) the power will be exercised by a minority smaller still. Man's conquest of Nature, if the dreams of some scientific planners are realized, means the rule of a few hundreds of men over billions upon billions of men. There neither is nor can be any simple increase of power on Man's side. Each new power won *by* man is a power *over* man as well. Each advance leaves him weaker as well as stronger. In every victory, beside being the general who triumphs, he is also the prisoner who follows the triumphal car.

Human Pain

WHEN OUR ANCESTORS referred to pains and sorrows as God's "vengeance" upon sin, they were not necessarily attributing evil passions to God; they may have been recognizing the good element in the idea of retribution. Until the evil man finds evil unmistakably present in his existence, in the form of pain, he is enclosed in illusion. Once pain has roused him, he knows that he is in some way or other "up against" the real universe: he either rebels (with the possibility of a clearer issue and deeper repentance at some later stage) or else makes some attempt at an adjustment, which, if pursued, will lead him to religion. It is true that neither effect is so certain now as it was in ages when the existence of God (or even of the Gods) was more widely known, but even in our own days we see it operating. Even atheists rebel and express, like Hardy and Housman, their rage against God although (or because) He does not in their view, exist: and other atheists, like Mr. Huxley, are driven by suffering to raise the whole problem of existence and to find some way of coming to terms with it which, if not Christian, is almost infinitely superior to fatuous content- ment with a profane life. No doubt Pain as God's mega- phone is a terrible instrument; it may lead to final and unre- pented rebellion. But it gives the only opportunity the bad man can have for amendment. It removes the veil; it plants the flag of truth within the fortress of a rebel soul.

If the first and lowest operation of pain shatters the illu- sion that all is well, the second shatters the illusion that what we have, whether good or bad in itself, is our own and enough for us. Everyone has noticed how hard it is to turn our thought to God when everything is going well with us. We "have all we want" is a terrible saying when "all" does not include God. We find God an interruption. As St. Augustine says somewhere, "God wants to give us something, but cannot, because our hands are full—there's nowhere for Him to put it." Or as a friend of mine said, "We regard God as an airman regards his parachute; it's there for emergencies but he hopes he'll never have to use it." Now God, who has made us, knows what we are and that our happiness lies in Him. Yet we will not seek it in Him as long as He leaves us any other resort where it can even plausibly be looked for. While what we call "our own life" remains agreeable, we will not surrender it to Him. What then can God do in our interests but make "our own life" less agreeable to us, and take away the plausible sources of false happiness? It is just here, where God's providence seems at first to be most cruel, that the Divine humility, the stooping down of the Highest, most deserves praise. We are perplexed to see misfortune falling upon decent, inoffensive, worthy people—on capable, hardworking mothers of families or diligent, thrifty little tradespeople, on those who have worked so hard, and so honestly, for their modest stock of happiness and now seem to be entering on the enjoyment of it with the fullest right. How can I say with sufficient tenderness what here needs to be said? It does not matter that I know I must become, in the eyes of every hostile reader, as it were, personally responsible for all the sufferings I try to explain—just as, to this day, everyone talks as if St. Augustine *wanted* unbaptized infants to go to Hell. But it matters enormously if I alienate anyone from the truth. Let me implore the reader to try to believe, if only for the moment, that God, who made these deserving people, may really be right when He thinks that their modest prosperity and the happiness of their children are not enough to make them blessed: that all this must fall from them in the end, and that if they have not learned to know Him, they will be wretched. And therefore He troubles them, warning them in advance of an insufficiency that one day they will have to discover. The life to themselves and their families stands between them and the recognition of their need; He makes that life less sweet to them.

Animal Pain

THE PROBLEM of animal suffering is appalling; not because the animals are so numerous . . . but because the Christian explanation of human pain cannot be extended to animal pain. So far as we know, beasts are incapable either of sin or virtue: therefore they can neither deserve pain nor be improved by it. . . . From the doctrine that God is good we may confidently deduce that the *appearance* of reckless divine cruelty in the animal kingdom is an illusion, and the fact that the only suffering we know at first hand (our own) turns out not to be a cruelty will make it easier to believe this. After that, everything is guesswork.

Suffering

ALL ARGUMENTS in justification of suffering provide bitter resentment against the author. You would like to know how I behave when I am experiencing pain, not writing books about it. You need not guess, for I will tell you; I am a great coward. But what is that to the purpose? When I think of pain—of anxiety that gnaws like fire and loneliness that spreads out like a desert, and the heartbreaking routine of monotonous misery, or again of dull aches that blacken our whole landscape or sudden nauseating pains that knock a man's heart out at one blow, of pains that seem already intolerable and then are suddenly increased, of infuriating scorpion-stinging pains that startle into maniacal movement a man who seems half dead with his previous tortures—it "quite o'ercrows my spirit." If I knew any way of escape I would crawl through sewers to find it. But what is the good of telling you about my feelings? You know them already: they are the same as yours. I am not arguing that pain is not painful. Pain hurts. That is what the word means. I am only trying to show that the old Christian doctrine of being made "perfect through suffering" (Hebrews 2:10) is not incredible. To prove it palatable is beyond my design.

In estimating the credibility of the doctrine two principles ought to be observed. In the first place, we must remember that the actual moment of present pain is only the center of what may be called the whole tribulational system which extends itself by fear and pity. Whatever good effects these experiences have are dependent upon the center; so that even if pain itself was of no spiritual value, yet, if fear and pity were, pain would have to exist in order that there should be something to be feared and pitied. And that fear and pity help us in our return to obedience and charity is not to be doubted. Everyone has experienced the effect of pity in making it easier for us to love the unlovely—that is, to love men not because they are in any way naturally agreeable to us but because they are our brethren. . . .

In the second place, when we are considering pain itself . . . we must be careful to attend to what we know and not to what we imagine. . . . About human pain we know, about animal pain we can only speculate. But even within the human race we must draw our evidence from instances that have come under our own observation. The tendency of this or that novelist or poet may represent suffering as wholly bad in its effects, as producing, and justifying, every kind of malice and brutality in the sufferer. And, of course, pain, like pleasure, can be so received: all that is given to a creature with free will must be two-edged, not by the nature of the giver or of the gift, but by the nature of the recipient. And, again, the evil results of pain can be multiplied if sufferers are persistently taught by the bystanders that such results are the proper and manly results for them to exhibit. Indignation at others' sufferings, though a generous passion, needs to be well managed lest it steal away patience and humility from those who suffer and plant anger and cynicism in their stead. But I am not convinced that suffering, if spared such officious vicarious indignation, has any natural tendency to produce such evils. I did not find the frontline trenches or the C.C.S. more full of hatred, selfishness, rebellion, and dishonesty than any other place. I have seen great beauty of spirit in some who were great sufferers. I have seen men, for the most part, grow better not worse with advancing years, and I have seen the last illness produce treasures of fortitude and meekness from most unpromising subjects. I see in loved and revered historical figures, such as Johnson and Cowper, traits which might scarcely have been tolerable if the men had been happier. If the world is indeed a "vale of soul-making," it seems on the whole to be doing its work.

The Crown and the Cross

MY MEMORIES of the last war haunted my dreams for years. Military service, to be plain, includes the threat of every *temporal* evil; pain and death which is what we fear from sickness: isolation from those we love which is what we fear from exile: toil under arbitrary masters, injustice, humiliation, which is what we fear from slavery: hunger, thirst, and exposure which is what we fear from poverty. I'm not a pacifist. If it's got to be, it's got to be. But the flesh is weak and selfish and I think death would be much better than to live through another war. Thank God He has not allowed my *faith* to be greatly tempted by the present horrors. I do not doubt that whatever misery He permits will be for our ultimate good unless by rebellious will we convert it to evil. But I get no further than Gethsemane: and am daily thankful that that scene of all others in our Lord's life did not go unrecorded. But what state of affairs in this world can we view with satisfaction? If we are unhappy, then we are unhappy. If we are happy, then we remember that the crown is not promised without the Cross and

tremble. In fact one comes to realize what one always admitted theoretically, that there is nothing here that will do
us good: the sooner we are safely out of this world the better. But "would it were evening, Hal, and all was well." I
have even (I'm afraid) caught myself wishing that I had
never been born, which is sinful. Also meaningless if you
think it out.

The process of living seems to consist in coming to realize
truths so ancient and simple that, if stated, they sound like
barren platitudes. They cannot sound otherwise to those
who have not had the relevant experience: that is why there
is no real teaching of such truths possible and every generation starts from scratch. . . .

Death

HUMAN DEATH, according to the Christians, is a result of a
human sin; Man, as originally created, was immune from it:
Man, when redeemed, and recalled to a new life (which
will, in some undefined sense, be a bodily life) in the midst
of a more organic and more fully obedient Nature, will be
immune from it again. This doctrine is, of course, simply
nonsense if a man is nothing but a Natural organism. But if
he were, then, as we have seen, all thoughts would be
equally nonsensical, for all would have irrational causes.
Man must therefore be a composite being—a natural organism tenanted by, or in a state of *symbiosis* with, a supernatural spirit. The Christian doctrine, startling as it must
seem to those who have not fully cleared their minds of
Naturalism, states that the relations which we now observe
between that spirit and that organism, are abnormal or
pathological ones. At present spirit can retain its foothold

against the incessant counterattacks of Nature (both physiological and psychological) only by perpetual vigilance, and physiological Nature always defeats it in the end. Sooner or later it becomes unable to resist the disintegrating processes at work in the body and death ensues. A little later the Natural organism (for it does not long enjoy its triumph) is similarly conquered by merely physical Nature and returns to the inorganic. But, on the Christian view, this was not always so. The spirit was once not a garrison, maintaining its post with difficulty in a hostile Nature, but was fully "at home" with its organism, like a king in his own country or a rider on his own horse—or better still, as the human part of a Centaur was "at home" with the equine part. Where spirit's power over the organism was complete and unresisted, death would never occur. No doubt, spirit's permanent triumph over natural forces which, if left to themselves, would kill the organism, would involve a continued miracle: but only the same sort of miracle which occurs every day—for whenever we think rationally we are, by direct spiritual power, forcing certain atoms in our brain and certain psychological tendencies in our natural soul to do what they would never have done if left to Nature. The Christian doctrine would be fantastic only if the present frontier situation between spirit and Nature in each human being were so intelligible and self-explanatory that we just "saw" it to be the only one that could ever have existed. But is it?

In reality the frontier situation is so odd that nothing but custom could make it seem natural, and nothing but the Christian doctrine can make it fully intelligible. There is certainly a state of war. But not a war of mutual destruction. Nature by dominating spirit wrecks all spiritual activities: Spirit by dominating Nature confirms and improves natural activities. The brain does not become less a brain by being used for rational thought. The emotions do not become weak or jaded by being organized in the service of a moral will—indeed they grow richer and stronger as a beard is strengthened by being shaved or a river is deepened by being banked. The body of the reasonable and virtuous man, other things being equal, is a better body than that of the fool or the debauchee, and his sensuous pleasures better simply as sensuous pleasures: for the slaves of the senses, after the first bait, are starved by their masters. Everything happens as if what we saw was not war, but rebellion: that rebellion of the lower against the higher by which the lower destroys both the higher and itself. And if the present situation is one of rebellion, then reason cannot reject but will rather demand the belief that there was a time before the rebellion broke out and may be a time after it has been settled. And if we thus see grounds for believing that the supernatural spirit and the natural organism in Man have quarreled, we shall immediately find it confirmed from two quite unexpected quarters.

Almost the whole of Christian theology could perhaps be deduced from the two facts (a) That men make coarse jokes, and (b) That they feel the dead to be uncanny. The coarse joke proclaims that we have here an animal which finds its own animality either objectionable or funny. Unless there had been a quarrel between the spirit and the organism, I do not see how this could be: it is the very mark of the two not being "at home" together. But it is very difficult to imagine such a state of affairs as original—to suppose a creature which from the very first was half shocked and half tickled to death at the mere fact of being the creature it is. I do not perceive that dogs see anything funny about being dogs: I suspect that angels see nothing funny about being angels. Our feeling about the dead is equally odd. It is idle to say that we dislike corpses because we are afraid of ghosts. You might say with equal truth that we fear ghosts and dislike corpses—for the ghost owes much of its horror to the associated ideas of pallor, decay, coffins, shrouds, and worms. In reality we hate the division which makes possible the conception of either corpse or ghost. Because the thing ought not to be divided, each of the halves into which it falls by division is detestable. The explanations which Naturalism gives both of bodily shame and of our feeling about the dead are not satisfactory. It refers us to primitive taboos and superstitions—as if these themselves were not obviously results of the thing to be explained. But once accept the Christian doctrine that man was originally a unity and that the present division is unnatural, and all the phenomena fall into place. It would be fantastic to suggest that the doctrine was devised to explain our enjoyment of a chapter in Rabelais, a good ghost story, or the *Tales* of Edgar Allan Poe. It does so nonetheless.

Judgment

IF THERE IS ANY THOUGHT at which a Christian trembles, it is the thought of God's "judgment." The "Day" of Judgment is "that day of wrath, that dreadful day." We pray to God to deliver us "in the hour of death and at the day of judgment." Christian art and literature for centuries have depicted its terrors. This note in Christianity certainly goes back to the teaching of Our Lord Himself; especially to the terrible parable of the Sheep and the Goats. This can leave no conscience untouched, for in it the "Goats" are condemned entirely for their sins of omission; as if to make us fairly sure that the heaviest charge against each of us turns not upon things he has done but on those he never did— perhaps never dreamed of doing.

It was therefore with great surprise that I first noticed how the Psalmists talk about the judgments of God. They talk like this: "O let the nations rejoice and be glad, for thou shalt judge the folk righteously" (Psalm 67:4), "Let the field be joyful . . . all the trees of the wood shall rejoice before the Lord, for he cometh, for he cometh to judge the earth" (Psalm 96:12,13). Judgment is apparently an occasion of universal rejoicing. People ask for it: "Judge me, O Lord my God, according to thy righteousness" (Psalm 35:24).

The reason for this soon becomes very plain. The ancient Jews, like ourselves, think of God's judgment in terms of an earthly court of justice. The difference is that the Christian pictures the case to be tried as a criminal case with himself as the plaintiff. The one hopes for acquittal, or rather for pardon; the other hopes for a resounding triumph with heavy damages. Hence he prays "judge my quarrel" or "avenge my cause" (Psalm 35:23). And though, as I said a minute ago, Our Lord in the parable of the Sheep and the Goats painted the characteristically Christian picture in another place, He is very characteristically Jewish. Notice what He means by "an unjust judge." By those words most of us would mean someone like Judge Jeffreys or the creatures who sat on the benches of German tribunals during the Nazi regime: someone who bullies witnesses and jurymen in order to convict, and then savagely to punish, innocent men. Once again, we are thinking of a criminal trial. We hope we shall never appear in the dock before such a judge. But the Unjust Judge in the parable is quite a different character. There is no danger of appearing in his court against your will: the difficulty is the opposite—to get into it. It is clearly a civil action. The poor woman (Luke 18:1–5) has had her little strip of land—room for a pigsty or a hen-run—taken away from her by a richer and more powerful neighbor (nowadays it would be Town Planners or some other "Body"). And she knows she has a perfectly watertight case. If once she could get it into court and have it tried by the laws of the land, she would be bound to get that strip back. But no one will listen to her, she can't get it tried. No wonder she is anxious for "judgment."

Behind this lies an age-old and almost worldwide experience which we have been spared. In most places and times it has been very difficult for the "small man" to get his case heard. The judge (and, doubtless, one or two of his underlings) has to be bribed. If you can't afford to "oil his palm," your case will never reach court. Our judges do not receive bribes. (We probably take this blessing too much for granted; it will not remain with us automatically). We need not therefore be surprised if the Psalms, and the Prophets, are full of longing for judgment, and regard the announcement that "judgment" is coming as good news. Hundreds of thousands of people who have been stripped of all they possess and who have the right entirely on their side will at last be heard. Of course, they are not afraid of judgment. They know their case is unanswerable—if only it could be heard. When God comes to judge, at last it will.

Resurrection of the Body

THE OLD PICTURE of the soul reassuming the corpse—perhaps blown to bits or long since usefully dissipated through nature—is absurd. Nor is it what St. Paul's words imply. And I admit that if you ask me what I substitute for this, I have only speculations to offer.

The principle behind these speculations is this. We are not, in this doctrine, concerned with matter as such at all; with waves and atoms and all that. What the soul cries out for is the resurrection of the senses. Even in this life matter would be nothing to us if it were not the source of sensations.

Now we already have some feeble and intermittent power

of raising dead sensations from their graves. I mean, of course, memory.

You see the way my thought is moving. But don't run away with the idea that when I speak of the resurrection of the body I mean merely that the blessed dead will have excellent memories of their sensuous experience on earth. I mean it the other way round: that memory as we now know it is a dim foretaste, a mirage even, of a power which the soul, or rather Christ in the soul (He went to "prepare a place" for us), will exercise hereafter. It need no longer be intermittent. Above all, it need no longer be private to the soul in which it occurs. . . .

At present we tend to think of the soul as somehow "inside" the body. But the glorified body of the resurrection as I conceive it—the sensuous life raised from its death—will be inside the soul. As God is not in space but space is in God. . . .

I don't say the resurrection of this body will happen at once. It may well be that this part of us sleeps in death, and the intellectual soul is sent to Lenten lands where she fasts in naked spirituality—a ghostlike and imperfectly human condition. I don't imply that an angel is a ghost. But naked spirituality is in accordance with His nature; not, I think, with ours. (A two-legged horse is maimed, but not a two-legged man.) Yet from that fast my hope is that we shall return and reassume the wealth we have laid down.

Then the new earth and sky, the same yet not the same as these, will rise in us as we have risen in Christ. And once again, after who knows what eons of the silence and the dark, the birds will sing and the waters flow, and lights and shadows move across the hills, and the faces of our friends laugh upon us with amazed recognition.

Guesses, of course, only guesses. If they are not true, something better will be. For "we know that we shall be made like Him, for we shall see Him as He is."

Purgatory

OUR SOULS *demand* Purgatory, don't they? Would it not break the heart if God said to us, "It is true, my son, that your breath smells and your rags drip with mud and slime, but we are charitable here and no one will upbraid you with these things, nor draw away from you. Enter into the joy"? Should we not reply, "With submission, sir, and if there is no objection, I'd *rather* be cleaned first." "It may hurt, you know"—"Even so, sir."

I assume that the process of purification will normally involve suffering. Partly from tradition; partly because most real good that has been done me in this life has involved it. But I don't think suffering is the purpose of the purgation. I can well believe that people neither much worse nor much better than I will suffer less than I or more. "No nonsense about merit." The treatment given will be the one required, whether it hurts little or much.

My favorite image on this matter comes from the dentist's chair. I hope that when the tooth of life is drawn and I am "coming round," a voice will say, "Rinse your mouth out with this." *This* will be a Purgatory.

Hell

I AM NOT GOING to try to prove the doctrine tolerable. Let us make no mistake; it is *not* tolerable. But I think the doctrine

can be shown to be moral by a critique of the objections ordinarily made, or felt, against it.

First, there is an objection, in many minds, to the idea of
retributive punishment as such. . . . Let us try to be honest
with ourselves. Picture to yourself a man who has risen to
wealth or power by a continued course of treachery and cruelty, by exploiting for purely selfish ends the noble motions
of his victims, laughing the while at their simplicity; who,
having thus attained success, uses it for the gratification of
lust and hatred and finally parts with the last rag of honor
among thieves by betraying his own accomplices and jeer-
ing at their last moments of bewildered disillusionment.
Suppose further, that he does all this, not (as we like to
imagine) tormented by remorse or even misgiving, but eating like a schoolboy and sleeping like a healthy infant—a
jolly, ruddy-cheeked man, without a care in the world, un-
shakably confident to the very end that he alone has found
the answer to the riddle of life, that God and man are fools
whom he has got the better of, that his way of life is utterly
successful, satisfactory, unassailable. We must be careful at
this point. The least indulgence of the passion for revenge
is very deadly sin. Christian charity counsels us to make
every effort for the conversion of such a man: to prefer his
conversion, at the peril of our own lives, perhaps of our
own souls, to his punishment; to prefer it infinitely. But
that is not the question. Supposing he *will* not be converted, what destiny in the eternal world can you regard as
proper for him? Can you really desire that such a man,
remaining what he is (and he must be able to do that if he
has free will) should be confirmed forever in his present
happiness—should continue, for all eternity, to be perfectly
convinced that the laugh is on his side? And if you cannot
regard this as tolerable, is it only your wickedness—only
spite—that prevents you from doing so? Or do you find that
conflict between Justice and Mercy, which has sometimes
seemed to you such an outmoded piece of theology, now

actually at work in your own mind, and feeling very much
as if it came to you from above, not from below? You are
moved, not by a desire for the wretched creature's pain as
such, but by a truly ethical demand that, soon or late, the
right should be asserted, the flag planted in this horribly
rebellious soul, even if no fuller and better conquest is to
follow. In a sense, it is better for the creature itself, even if
it never becomes good, that it should know itself a failure, a
mistake. Even mercy can hardly wish to such a man his
eternal, contented continuance in such ghastly illusion.
Thomas Aquinas said of suffering, as Aristotle had said of
shame, that it was a thing not good in itself, but a thing
which might have a certain goodness in particular circumstances. That is to say, if evil is present, pain at recognition
of the evil, being a kind of knowledge, is relatively good;
for the alternative is that the soul should be ignorant of the
evil, or ignorant that the evil is contrary to its nature, "either of which," says the philosopher, "is *manifestly* bad."
And I think, though we tremble, we agree. . . .

Another objection turns on the apparent disproportion
between eternal damnation and transitory sin. And if we
think of eternity as a mere prolongation of time, it is dis-
proportionate. But many would reject this idea of eternity.
If we think of time as a line—which is a good image, because the parts of time are successive and no two of them
can coexist; that is, there is no *width* in time, only length—
we probably ought to think of eternity as a plane or even a
solid. Thus the whole reality of a human being would be
represented by a solid figure. That solid would be mainly
the work of God, acting through grace and nature, but
human free will would have contributed the base line
which we call earthly life: and if you draw your base line
askew, the whole solid will be in the wrong place. The fact
that life is short, or, in the symbol, that we contribute only
one little line to the whole complex figure, might be
regarded as a Divine mercy. For even if the drawing of that

little line, left to our free will, is sometimes so badly done as
to spoil the whole, how much worse a mess might we have
made of the figure if more had been entrusted to us? . . .

A third objection turns on the frightful intensity of the
pains of Hell as suggested by medieval art and, indeed, by
certain passages in Scripture. Von Hügel here warns us not
to confuse the doctrine itself with the *imagery* by which it
may be conveyed. Our Lord speaks of Hell under three
symbols: first, that of punishment ("everlasting punishment," Matthew 25:46); second, that of destruction ("fear
Him who is able to destroy both body and soul in hell,"
Matthew 10:28); and thirdly, that of privation, exclusion, or
banishment into "the darkness outside," as in the parables
of the man without a wedding garment or of the wise and
foolish virgins. The prevalent idea of fire is significant because it combines the ideas of torment and destruction.
Now it is quite certain that all these expressions are intended to suggest something unspeakably horrible, and any
interpretation which does not face that fact is, I am afraid,
out of court from the beginning. But it is not necessary to
concentrate on the images of torture to the exclusion of
those suggesting destruction and privation. What can that
be whereof all three images are equally proper symbols?
Destruction, we should naturally assume, means the un-
making, or cessation, of the destroyed. And people often
talk as if the "annihilation" of a soul were intrinsically possible. In all our experience, however, the destruction of one
thing means the emergence of something else. Burn a log,
and you have gases, heat, and ash. To *have been* a log
means now being those three things. If soul can be destroyed, must there not be a state of *having been* a human
soul? And is not that, perhaps, the state which is equally
well described as torment, destruction, and privation? . . .

A fourth objection is that no charitable man could himself
be blessed in Heaven while he knew that even one human
soul was still in Hell; and if so, are we more merciful than

God? At the back of this objection lies a mental picture of Heaven and Hell coexisting in unilinear time as the histories of England and America coexist: so that at each moment the blessed could say "The miseries of Hell are *now* going on." But I notice that Our Lord, while stressing the terror of Hell with unsparing severity, usually emphasizes the idea, not of duration but of *finality*. Consignment to the destroying fire is usually treated as the end of the story— not as the beginning of a new story. That the lost soul is eternally fixed in its diabolical attitude we cannot doubt: but whether this eternal fixity implies endless duration—or duration at all—we cannot say. . . .

Finally, it is objected that the ultimate loss of a single soul means the defeat of omnipotence. And so it does. In creating beings with free will, omnipotence from the outset submits to the possibility of such defeat. What you call defeat, I call miracle: for to make things which are not Itself, and thus to become, in a sense, capable of being resisted by its own handiwork, is the most astonishing and unimaginable of all the feats we attribute to the Deity. I willingly believe that the damned are, in one sense, successful, rebels to the end; that the doors of Hell are locked on the *inside*. I do not mean that the ghosts may not *wish* to come out of Hell, in the vague fashion wherein an envious man "wishes" to be happy: but they certainly do not will even the first preliminary stages of that self-abandonment through which alone the soul can reach any good. They enjoy forever the horrible freedom they have demanded, and are therefore self-enslaved just as the blessed, forever submitting to obedience, become through all eternity more and more free.

Heaven

SCRIPTURE AND TRADITION habitually put the joys of Heaven into the scale against the sufferings of earth, and no solution of the problem of pain which does not do so can be called a Christian one. We are very shy nowadays of even mentioning Heaven. We are afraid of the jeer about "pie in the sky," and of being told that we are trying to "escape" from the duty of making a happy world here and now into dreams of a happy world elsewhere. But either there is "pie in the sky" or there is not. If there is not, then Christianity is false, for this doctrine is woven into its whole fabric. If there is, then this truth, like any other, must be faced, whether it is useful at political meetings or no. Again, we are afraid that Heaven is a bribe, and that if we make it our goal we shall no longer be disinterested. It is not so. Heaven offers nothing that a mercenary soul can desire. It is safe to tell the pure in heart that they shall see God, for only the pure in heart want to. There are rewards that do not sully motives. A man's love for a woman is not mercenary because he wants to marry her, nor his love for poetry mercenary because he wants to read it, nor his love of exercise less disinterested because he wants to run and leap and walk. Love, by definition, seeks to enjoy its object.

✳

I do *not* think that the life of Heaven bears any analogy to play or dance in respect of frivolity. I do think that while we are in this "valley of tears," cursed with labor, hemmed round with necessities, tripped up with frustrations, doomed to perpetual plannings, puzzlings, and anxieties, certain qualities that must belong to the celestial condition have no chance to get through, can project no image of themselves, except in activities which, for us here and now, are frivolous. For surely we must suppose the life of the blessed to be an end in itself, indeed The End: to be utterly spontaneous; to be the complete reconciliation of boundless freedom with order—with the most delicately adjusted, supple, intricate, and beautiful order? How can you find any image of this in the "serious" activities either of our natural or of our (present) spiritual life? Either in our precariousness and heartbroken affections or in the Way which is always, in some degree, a *via crucis?* No. . . . It is only in our "hours off," only in our moments of permitted festivity, that we find an analogy. Dance and game *are* frivolous, unimportant down here; for "down here" is not their natural place. Here, they are a moment's rest from the life we were placed here to live. But in this world everything is upside down. That which, if it could be prolonged here, would be a truancy, is likest that which in a better country is the End of Ends. Joy is the serious business of Heaven.

Bibliography

BOOKS QUOTED IN THE TEXT

The Abolition of Man: Reflections on Education with Special Reference to the Teaching of English in the Upper Forms of Schools.
    London: Geoffrey Bles, 1946.
    New York: Macmillan Publishing Co., Inc., 1947.
    New York: Macmillan Paperback, 1965.
Christian Reflections. Edited by Walter Hooper.
    Grand Rapids: W. B. Eerdmans Publishing Co., 1967.
The Four Loves.
    London: Geoffrey Bles, 1960.
    New York: Harcourt Brace Jovanovich, 1960.
    New York: HBJ Paperback, 1971.
God in the Dock: Essays in Theology and Ethics. Edited, with a Preface, by Walter Hooper.
    London: Geoffrey Bles, 1970; published as *Undeceptions.*
    Grand Rapids: W. B. Eerdmans Publishing Co., 1970.

A Grief Observed.
> London: Faber and Faber Limited, 1961. Published under the pseudonym N. W. Clerk.
> New York: The Seabury Press, Inc., 1963. Published under the pseudonym N. W. Clerk.
> New York: Bantam Books, 1976. Published under the name C. S. Lewis, with an Afterword by Chad Walsh.

Letters of C. S. Lewis. Edited, with a Memoir, by W. H. Lewis.
> London: Geoffrey Bles, 1975.
> New York: Harcourt Brace Jovanovich, 1975.
> New York: HBJ Paperback, 1975.

Letters to an American Lady. Edited by Clyde Kilby.
> Grand Rapids: W. B. Eerdmans Publishing Co., 1967.
> New York: Pyramid Books, 1971.

Letters to Malcolm: Chiefly on Prayer.
> London: Geoffrey Bles, 1964.
> New York: Harcourt Brace Jovanovich, 1964.
> New York: HBJ Paperback, 1973.

Mere Christianity. A revised and enlarged edition, with a new introduction, of the three books *The Case for Christianity* (London: Geoffrey Bles, 1942; New York: Macmillan, 1943), *Christian Behavior* (London: Geoffrey Bles, 1943; New York: Macmillan, 1943), and *Beyond Personality* (London: Geoffrey Bles, 1944; New York: Macmillan, 1945).
> London: Geoffrey Bles, 1952.
> New York: Macmillan Publishing Co., Inc., 1952.
> New York: Macmillan Paperback, 1960.

Miracles: A Preliminary Study.
> London: Geoffrey Bles, 1947.
> New York: Macmillan Publishing Co., Inc., 1947.
> New York: Macmillan Paperback, 1963.

The Problem of Pain.
> London: Geoffrey Bles, 1940.
> New York: Macmillan Publishing Co., Inc., 1943.
> New York: Macmillan Paperback, 1962.

Reflections on the Psalms.
> London: Geoffrey Bles, 1958.
> New York: Harcourt Brace Jovanovich, 1958.
> New York: HBJ Paperback, 1964.

The Screwtape Letters.
> London: Geoffrey Bles, 1942.

New York: Macmillan Publishing Co., Inc., 1943.

New York: Macmillan Paperback, 1959.

The Screwtape Letters, with Screwtape Proposes a Toast. With a new
and additional Preface.

New York: Macmillan Publishing Co., Inc., 1964.

New York: Macmillan Paperback, 1962.

Undeceptions. See *God in the Dock.*

Transposition. See *The Weight of Glory.*

The Weight of Glory and Other Addresses.

London: Geoffrey Bles, 1949; published as *Transposition
and Other Addresses.*

New York: Macmillan Publishing Co., Inc., 1949.

Grand Rapids: W. B. Eerdmans Publishing Co., 1965.

The World's Last Night and Other Essays.

New York: Harcourt Brace Jovanovich, 1960.

New York: HBJ Paperback, 1973.

BOOKS NOT QUOTED IN THE TEXT

The Allegory of Love: A Study in Medieval Tradition.

London: Oxford University Press, 1936, 1938.

New York: OUP Paperback, 1958.

The Chronicles of Narnia. Boxed set of 7 paperbacks.

New York: Collier Books, 1970.

The Dark Tower and Other Stories. Edited, and with a Preface, by
Walter Hooper.

London: Collins Publishers, 1977.

New York: Harcourt Brace Jovanovich, 1977.

*The Discarded Image: An Introduction to Medieval and Renaissance
Literature.*

Cambridge: Cambridge University Press, 1964.

Dymer.

London: J. M. Dent, 1926; published under the pseu-
donym Clive Hamilton.

New York: E. P. Dutton, 1926.

New York: Macmillan Publishing Co., Inc., 1950.

English Literature in the Sixteenth Century, Excluding Drama.

Oxford: Clarendon Press, 1954.

An Experiment in Criticism.

Cambridge: Cambridge University Press, 1961.

The Great Divorce.
    London: Geoffrey Bles, 1945.
    New York: Macmillan Publishing Co., Inc., 1946.
    New York: Macmillan Paperback, 1963.
The Horse and His Boy. Book 5 in *The Chronicles of Narnia.* Illustrated by Pauline Baynes.
    London: The Bodley Head, 1956.
    New York: Macmillan Publishing Co., Inc., 1954.
    New York: Collier Books, 1970.
The Last Battle. Book 7 in *The Chronicles of Narnia.* Illustrated by Pauline Baynes.
    London: The Bodley Head, 1956.
    New York: Macmillan Publishing Co., Inc., 1956.
    New York: Collier Books, 1970.
The Lion, The Witch, and The Wardrobe. Book 1 in *The Chronicles of Narnia.* Illustrated by Pauline Baynes.
    London: Geoffrey Bles, 1950.
    New York: Macmillan Publishing Co., Inc., 1950.
    New York: Collier Books, 1970.
The Magician's Nephew. Book 6 in *The Chronicles of Narnia.* Illustrated by Pauline Baynes.
    London: The Bodley Head, 1955.
    New York: Macmillan Publishing Co., Inc., 1955.
    New York: Collier Books, 1970.
A Mind Awake: An Anthology of C. S. Lewis. Edited by Clyde S. Kilby.
    New York: Harcourt Brace Jovanovich, 1968.
Narrative Poems. Edited by Walter Hooper.
    London: Geoffrey Bles, 1969.
    New York: Harcourt Brace Jovanovich, 1972.
Of Other Worlds: Essays and Stories. Edited, with a Preface, by Walter Hooper.
    New York: Harcourt Brace Jovanovich, 1966.
    New York: HBJ Paperback, 1975.
Out of the Silent Planet. Book 1 of *The Space Trilogy.*
    London: John Lane, 1938.
    New York: Macmillan Publishing Co., Inc., 1943.
    New York: Macmillan Paperback, 1965.
Perelandra. Book 2 of *The Space Trilogy.*
    London: John Lane, 1943.
    New York: Macmillan Publishing Co., Inc., 1944.
    New York: Macmillan Paperback, 1965.

The Pilgrim's Regress: An Allegorical Apology for Christianity, Reason, and Romanticism.
    London: J. M. Dent, 1933.
    New York: Sheed and Ward, 1935.
    With the author's important new Preface on Romanticism, footnotes, and running headlines.
    London: Geoffrey Bles, 1943.
    New York: Sheed and Ward, 1944.
    Grand Rapids: W. B. Eerdmans Publishing Co., 1958.

A Preface to "Paradise Lost."
    New York: Oxford University Press, 1942.
    London: Oxford University Press, 1942.

Poems. Edited by Walter Hooper.
    London: Geoffrey Bles, 1964.
    New York: Harcourt Brace Jovanovich, 1965.

Prince Caspian. Book 2 in *The Chronicles of Narnia.* Illustrated by Pauline Baynes.
    London: Geoffrey Bles, 1951.
    New York: Macmillan Publishing Co., Inc., 1951.
    New York: Collier Books, 1970.

Rehabilitations and Other Essays.
    Oxford, London: Oxford University Press, 1934.

Selected Literary Essays.
    Cambridge, London: Cambridge University Press, 1969.

The Silver Chair. Book 4 in *The Chronicles of Narnia.* Illustrated by Pauline Baynes.
    London: Geoffrey Bles, 1953.
    New York: Macmillan Publishing Co., Inc., 1953.
    New York: Collier Books, 1970.

The Space Trilogy. Boxed paperback set of *Out of the Silent Planet, Perelandra,* and *That Hideous Strength.*
    New York: Macmillan Paperback, 1975.

Spenser's Images of Life.
    Cambridge, London: Cambridge University Press, 1967.

Studies in Words.
    Cambridge: Cambridge University Press, 1960; second edition, 1966.

That Hideous Strength. Book 3 of *The Space Trilogy.*
    London: John Lane, 1945.
    New York: Macmillan Publishing Co., Inc., 1946.
    New York: Macmillan Paperback, 1965.

They Asked for a Paper.
London: Geoffrey Bles, 1962.
Till We Have Faces: A Myth Retold.
London: Geoffrey Bles, 1956.
New York: Harcourt Brace Jovanovich, 1957.
Grand Rapids: WBE Paperback, 1966.
The Voyage of the "Dawn Treader." Book 3 of *The Chronicles of Narnia.* Illustrated by Pauline Baynes.
London: Geoffrey Bles, 1952.
New York: Macmillan Publishing Co., Inc., 1952.
New York: Collier Books, 1970.

BOOKS ABOUT C. S. LEWIS

Arnott, Anne. *The Secret Country of C. S. Lewis.* Illustrated by Patricia Frost.
Grand Rapids: W. B. Eerdmans Publishing Co., 1975.
Carnell, Corbin Scott. *Bright Shadow of Reality: C. S. Lewis and the Feeling Intellect.*
Grand Rapids: W. B. Eerdmans Publishing Co., 1974.
Gibb, Jocelyn, ed. *Light on C. S. Lewis.* Essays by Owen Barfield, Austin Farrer, J. A. W. Bennett, Nevill Coghill, John Lawlor, Stella Gibbons, Kathleen Raine, Chad Walsh, Walter Hooper.
London: Geoffrey Bles, 1965.
New York: HBJ Harvest Book, 1976.
Gilbert, Douglas and Kilby, Clyde S. *C. S. Lewis: Images of His World.*
Grand Rapids: W. B. Eerdmans Publishing Co., 1973.
Green, Roger Lancelyn and Hooper, Walter. *C. S. Lewis: A Biography.*
New York: Harcourt Brace Jovanovich, 1974.
Holmer, Paul L. *C. S. Lewis: The Shape of His Faith and Thought.*
New York: Harper & Row, 1976.
Keefe, Carolyn, ed. *C. S. Lewis: Speaker and Teacher.* Foreword by Thomas Howard. Grand Rapids: Zondervan Publishing House, 1971.
Kilby, Clyde S. *The Christian World of C. S. Lewis.*
Grand Rapids: W. B. Eerdmans Publishing Co., 1964.
Lindskoog, Kathryn Ann. *C. S. Lewis: Mere Christian.* Foreword by Clyde S. Kilby.
Glendale, Ca.: G/L Publications, 1973.
———. *The Lion of Judah in Never-Never Land: The Theology*

of C. S. Lewis Expressed in His Fantasies for Children. With
a Preface by Walter Hooper.

Grand Rapids: W. B. Eerdmans Publishing Co., 1973.

Montgomery, John Warwick, ed. Myth, Allegory, and Gospel: An
Interpretation of J. R. R. Tolkien, C. S. Lewis, G. K. Chesterton,
Charles Williams. Essays by Edmund Fuller, Clyde S. Kilby,
Russell Kirk, John W. Montgomery, and Chad Walsh.

Minneapolis: Bethany Fellowship, Inc., 1974.

Schakel, Peter J., Editor. The Longing for a Form: Essays on the Fiction of C. S. Lewis.

Kent, Ohio: Kent State University Press, 1977.

Walsh, Chad. C. S. Lewis: Apostle to the Skeptics.

New York: Macmillan Publishing Co., Inc., 1949.

Folcraft, Pa.: Folcraft Library Editions, 1974.

Sources

The page numbers cited below refer to the paperback editions of C. S. Lewis's works currently available in American bookstores.